CUTTING COSTS

CUTTING COSTS

An Executive's Guide to Increased Profits

Harry E. Figgie, Jr.

Foreword by John S. R. Shad

amacom

American Management Association

Library of Congress Cataloging-in-Publication Data

Figgie, Harry E.
    Cutting Costs: An Executive's Guide to Increased Profits
    Harry E. Figgie Jr. : foreword by John S. R. Shad.—1st AMACOM pbk.
    ed.
        p.   cm.
    ISBN 0-8144-7720-8
        1. Cost control. I. Shad, John S. R., 1923–   . II. Title.
    III. Title: Cutting Costs: An Executive's Guide to Increased Profits
        HD47.3.F55   1990
658.15'5—dc20   89-17763
                                                                      CIP

First AMACOM paperback edition 1990.
Originally published by Probus Publishing Company.

Printing number

10 9 8 7 6 5 4 3 2 1

This book represents a lifetime of experience and therefore is dedicated:

first, to my mother and father who served as an inspiration and who firmly believed in, and taught me to believe in, the American system;

second, to the many executives like Dale Coenen, Ed Burnell, Ed Morris, George Herzog, Don Bryant, Morris Hartman, Shep Cornell, Hank Ormerod, Charlie Moore, Don Harbaugh, Ed Hedner, and countless others who took an interest in my career and trained or helped me at its crucial points;

and third, to my wife Nancy and to my three sons whose patience and understanding have permitted me to succeed.

Contents

Appendixes

Foreword

I have known Harry Figgie since we were classmates at the Harvard Business School in the late 1940s. I have observed, sometimes at close hand and other times from afar, his extraordinary accomplishments in manufacturing, sales, consulting, and overall industrial management. I watched him take a tiny company, on the verge of bankruptcy, and build it into one of the nation's leading fully integrated producers of fire protection equipment—everything from sprinklers and brass work to fire engines. And this is but one of the several successful areas of Figgie International today.

Harry was once described to me as the best cost reduction expert in the United States. I know of no one whose depth of knowledge and demonstrated results approach his in this critical aspect of corporate management.

Harry Figgie has an intense dedication to the advancement of management techniques. He feels a strong responsibility to share his proven knowledge with future generations. So much so that his share of this book's profits is going to charity.

This book describes his unique commonsense approach to cost reduction. You will find it a fascinating, informative, and thought-provoking experience. It is a unique, important contribution to the state of the art of corporate management.

John S. R. Shad
former Chairman of the
Securities and Exchange Commission

Preface

I have been very fortunate during the past forty years to have had a wide variety of business experiences. After spending the beginning of my career performing industrial operating assignments both in manufacturing and in sales, the next nine years were spent specializing in reorganization and cost reduction at a leading consulting firm. During this period of time I closely observed more than five hundred companies, and it became evident to me that there are certain fundamental approaches to reducing costs that transcend virtually all industrial operations.

Later, as a group vice-president of a large corporation, and subsequently as head of a medium-size company ($20 million) which has grown over the years into a $1 billion corporation consisting of forty divisions, and as the head of a small family corporation which has grown in sales from $250,000 to roughly $25 million, I have been able to use my cost reduction training to great advantage. As a result of this fortunate combination of experience and training. I have developed an approach to profit improvement that can be remarkably successful in reducing costs, and thereby improving profit, within most small to medium-size companies. To the best of my knowledge, a number of these techniques have never been seen in print. They certainly have never been collected into a comprehensive, workable guide. Hence my decision to write this book.

Acknowledgments

As indicated in the dedication, this book is the result of a lifetime of business experience. There are certain people, however, who have helped me in putting these experiences down on paper.

For their help in reviewing particular chapters, I would like to thank the following Figgie International executives: Richard G. Bezjak, President of the Kersey and American LaFrance divisions; Richard H. DeLisle, Manager of Training; Donald E. Eagon, Vice President of Public Affairs; Maynard R. Shope, retired Director of Manufacturing; Joseph J. Skadra, Vice President and Controller; Lane W. Thorson, retired Director of Market and Product Planning; and Mike Trbovich, Group Vice President. I would also like to thank C. Willard Bryant, retired General Electric procurement executive. My son Dr. Harry E. Figgie III's comprehensive review of the entire document once the first draft was completed was invaluable.

Special thanks to Adam Snyder for his tremendous assistance in preparing and helping me to organize the various drafts of this manuscript. He has the patience of Job.

Introduction

The first point to remember about the concept of cost reduction is that it can be used interchangeably with the term "profit improvement." If profit improvement is the glass of water half full, then cost reduction is the glass of water half empty.

Nevertheless, it is remarkable how often a comprehensive cost reduction program is neglected even when the company's president or chief executive officer (CEO) is doing everything else possible to increase profits. Chief executives often are so busy with their day-to-day operations that they feel they simply do not have the time to implement vitally important cost reductions. The irony is that there is no more cost-effective way in which a top executive can spend time. Regardless of the current position in the business cycle, cost reduction should be one of the first recourses of management when attempting to improve or stabilize profit. Chief executives should not wait until a stressful economic period to realize that reducing costs can immediately and effectively improve a company's bottom line performance. Delaying cost reduction can be suicidal.

There are many reasons why cost reduction is neglected as a strategy to improve profits. In the first place, it is often thought of as a dirty business. No executive wants to be the one to trim the fat if it means eliminating part of the work force. And few executives are willing to call an entire department into their office and tell employees that they have been performing inefficiently for the past five, ten, or twenty years.

In addition, profit improvement through cost reduction is not as flashy or dramatic as, say, a large increase in sales, even though cost reduction is much more beneficial to a company's bottom line. A 30 percent increase in a company's sales might make the front page of a newspaper's business section; a comparable reduction in costs surely would not receive the same favorable treatment, but it would use a lot less cash and assets and have a much more favorable impact on the company's bottom line and/or its competitive position.

Another reason why executives are reluctant to initiate a comprehensive cost reduction program is that very few of them know where to begin. While most managers have considerable skills in their original areas of expertise, few have ever received instruction or had experience in comprehensive cost reduction analysis and corrective techniques.

Regardless of the background of men and women in top management—sales, production, legal, accounting, purchasing, or administration—rarely are they taught how to trim fat, eliminate waste, and tighten the overall, coordinated operation. Despite the vital need for cost reduction analysis, so basic to good corporate management, cost reduction methods are seldom taught in business schools even at the graduate level, and the details and tremendous benefits of cost reduction are rarely discussed at business conferences or seminars. If the importance of cost reduction is not emphasized at the top, management cannot expect lower-level executives to create, implement, or maintain profit-improving cost reduction techniques. At Figgie International, for example, we almost always put cost reduction on the agenda at our annual presidents' meetings.

Lack of knowledge, in other words, coupled with lack of time and the day-to-day pressures of a chief executive's normal operations, makes cost reduction one of the most neglected areas of management, and one of the more difficult areas of management acumen. It is the one area in which the executive cannot be the "good guy." It is the area that most executives tend to avoid.

The Harry Figgie Guide to Cost Reduction and Profit Improvement is intended to fill this unrecognized yet extremely damaging gap in the educational and professional experience of most top executives. The handbook is aimed at heads of small to medium-size companies and their divisions. In some shape or form, many of the techniques described in this text are also applicable to larger companies and central headquarters. It is important to keep in mind that while a prototypic company doing, say, $5 million in annual sales may be used to illustrate a certain cost reduction principle, in virtually every case that same principle can be applied to a $50, $100, $200 million, or even larger company.

Regardless of a company's size, by following the methods described in this text, the goal should be a 10 percent across-the-board savings, although in many cases 20 to 30 percent is in fact attainable. As will be demonstrated, a 10 percent reduction in costs can increase profits by 25 to 50 percent, or more if the savings can be preserved, which in and of itself is frequently a problem. Because the multifaceted benefits of cost reduction are often not fully recognized by many executives, this book details various cost reduction techniques, as well as the cost savings and profit improvements that can be realized.

Before beginning this text, the reader should understand that this is a cost reduction *primer*. Although it discusses in depth the components of a comprehensive cost reduction program, it will not turn an untrained executive into an instant expert. It will, however, clearly demonstrate the theories behind the most important cost reduction techniques, and the impact they can have on a company's profitability. A single reading of Chapter 3's discussion of work sampling, for example, may not immediately enable an executive to direct a complicated work sampling operation personally. It will, however, demonstrate to the executive the goals, guidelines, benefits, and specific procedures of work sampling. Only then will an executive be able to direct an industrial engineer or outside consultant to establish an effective, ongoing program.

In a similar vein, this book emphasizes several key cost reduction tenets that apply to all phases of a comprehensive program. The greater value of cost reduction as opposed to growth, for example, is demonstrated in detail in Chapter 4, but implied, if not emphasized, in virtually every chapter. The reader is repeatedly reminded that increasing sales makes it necessary for a company to find money in order to provide precious working capital, while cost reduction costs virtually nothing. A dollar saved is a dollar added to the company's bottom line. An additional dollar of sales, on the other hand, may or may not be favorably reflected in the profit and loss statement. In order to generate this dollar increase, any number of expenses will be increased which may even cost the company more than the additional dollar earned. Perhaps it should not be surprising how few U.S. business executives truly understand the ramifications of this basic truth, since they have been trained to believe that sales growth should be their number one priority.

Another profit improvement technique emphasized throughout this text is concentrating the bulk of cost reduction efforts in the areas that affect profit the most. The purchasing department, for example, is frequently responsible for as much as half the sales dollar, but is often relegated to an expediting function and shielded from top management by several layers of corporate structure. The importance of developing an efficient, cost-conscious purchasing department reporting directly to the chief executive officer cannot be overemphasized.

The Harry Figgie Guide to Cost Reduction and Profit Improvement is deliberately structured so that the busy executive can immediately launch an effective cost reduction program. Part 1, consisting of the first three chapters, offers instructions for the first weekend, the first week, and the first month, respectively. All told, this constitutes a thirty-day "quick and dirty" program which should result in immediate and considerable rewards and pay for subsequent cost reduction efforts. Part II establishes cost reduction priorities, and Part III offers specific cost reduction techniques in a variety of departmental areas.

It is the thesis of this primer that industrial operations, like human beings, acquire bad habits, and that the company that is not subject to continuing cost reduction analysis may be assumed to be operating at less than peak efficiency and therefore earning less than its maximum potential profit. Industrial operations not only require periodic checkups, but constant and diligent surveillance in order to assure that inefficient, wasteful, or damaging habits, once corrected, do not return. A cost reduction program is not a one-shot approach for *effecting* economies. It should be conducted on a continuing basis so that the techniques become second nature to all top-level executives. A full-scale cost reduction program repeated a year later will almost always yield substantial additional savings, frequently equal to the initial savings of a year earlier.

Only by practicing the simple cost reduction techniques detailed on the following pages can CEOs of small or medium-size manufacturing companies have the satisfaction of knowing that their companies are operating at close to peak efficiency and maximum profitability. All it takes is a willingness to learn and a determination to change management style to make cost reduction a continuing top priority. Cost reducion must become a way of life to the American corporate executive. It must become a thought process that is continually applied and reapplied.

I

The First Month

1

The First Weekend— Organizational Analysis

Any effective cost reduction program must include both a short-term and a long-term approach. Neither tactic will ultimately be successful without the other.

Completion of a short-term strategy, which may be identified as the "quick and dirty" (q and d) method, can be accomplished in just one month. The savings that can be achieved in these first thirty days are substantial, and will more than pay for further, more in-depth, longer-term cost reduction measures to be discussed in Part II.

The "quick and dirty" thirty-day method utilizes three techniques which, if followed, can result in a 5 to 20 percent reduction in personnel costs (with 10 percent a reasonable target) within a month's time. The three basic steps are:

1. Organizational analysis

2. Ratio analysis

3. Work sampling

The first step, organizational analysis, can be initiated during any weekend in the comfort and privacy of one's own home. The only reference material that will be needed is an accurate, up-to-date organization chart that includes the salaries of each employee. Ratio analysis can subsequently be accomplished in the first week, to be followed by work sampling during the balance of the month.

The object of an organizational analysis is to determine how company departments can be streamlined and reorganized in such a way as to not only cut costs, but also increase effectiveness and productivity. It may be, for example, that some of your managers have too much responsibility while others don't have enough. Or perhaps those responsible for committing the bulk of your company's money are too isolated from the top executive responsible for the company's bottom line performance.

No one in your entire salaried organization should be overlooked in an organizational analysis—from the chief executive, down through the foremen, to each department, to the most junior person on the sales force. At first this may seem like an impossible assignment. But remember, we are dealing with small and medium-size companies, not giants. And even for huge companies, organizational analyses can successfully be conducted for divisions, departments, and corporate headquarters.

Organizational analysis for most companies can be so simple and so effective that, along with the other two phases of your "q and d" method, it should be repeated at least once a year. It can be undertaken with the knowledge that your operation, if it is at all typical, can stand a great deal of organizational tightening—tightening that can be accomplished during one weekend, sitting in your most comfortable armchair.

Three Important Rules

Before taking a look at your own organizational chart or the sample charts presented in this chapter, you must be able to recognize and implement three very basic, but often broken, organizational rules:

1. *Span of control.* An executive should supervise no more than ten employees, but no less than seven.

2. *Proper reporting level.* The executives responsible for the departments that can most affect profits should report directly to the head of the company.

3. *Management insulation.* The number of management levels between the company head and the lowest level of supervision should be kept to an absolute minimum.

These rules may seem simple, but in most corporations they are all too often either overlooked or ignored.

In administration, *the span of control for an executive should be from seven to ten persons.* With fewer than seven persons to supervise, executives may not be fully utilizing their time or abilities; with more than ten persons to supervise, they may be spreading themselves too thin and may thus inadvertently, or through neglect, add to costs. However, in the shop one foreman can maintain control of up to fifteen persons in a complicated operation, and up to fifty or more in a simple operation.

Not only is it important to make certain that executives are supervising the optimum number of employees, it is equally important that these executives are themselves reporting to the *proper* person. Time and again I have witnessed situations in which a chief executive officer has no direct control over the departments that influence profits the most. In keeping with our first rule concerning span of control, generally no more than seven to ten executives should report directly to the CEO, but included among these seven to ten executives should usually be the director of sales, director of manufacturing, director of purchasing, the controller, the director of industrial relations, and the director of engineering. This still leaves one to four positions open, to be tailored to your own specific operation. These guidelines assume, of course, a profit center operation as opposed to a corporate headquarters of a multidivision company.

The person who is probably most often left off this list is the one person who should virtually always report directly to the head of the company: the director of the purchasing department. The director of purchasing often controls as much as 50 percent of the sales dollar and therefore has a very substantial impact on a company's bottom line performance. A 10 percent reduction in purchasing costs can mean a 5 percent increase in profits, while a 10 percent reduction in labor costs will probably translate into less than a 1 percent increase in profits (see Chapter 4).

Despite the tremendous importance of purchasing, many companies nevertheless allow the purchasing chief to report to the plant manager (or even to the assistant plant manager), or quite frequently to a materials manager, who in turn frequently reports to someone below the level of president. Purchasing is often mistakenly put under manufacturing or combined with inventory and production control. (This is generally a one over two organization and isolates a key department from the chief executive.)

If the purchasing department is being short-shrifted, it is an immediate indication that your organization needs an extensive reanalysis. The importance of the purchasing department cannot possibly be overemphasized, and will be discussed repeatedly throughout this guide. In addition, specific techniques to reduce costs in the purchasing area will be detailed in Chapters 6 and 7.

Other executives, the head of industrial relations, for example, should also report directly to the chief executive officer for much the same reasons. Industrial relations no longer merely involves the function of hiring the right people and keeping them happy and productive. It involves insurance, compensation, retirement benefits, labor negotiations, personnel, equal opportunity, safety, and a host of other costly functions, including budget-gobbling fringe benefits which can total up to 40 percent of your factory burden and an even greater percentage of your salary and wage costs.

Case Study: Manufacturing Organization

As a first step toward reorganizing your own organizational chart, study Exhibit 1–1, the manufacturing organizational chart for a typical metals fabricating company. Consider how you would make your organization more effective and responsive by streamlining it and eliminating the excess. As you begin, be certain to keep in mind the three rules discussed earlier in this chapter. Seek to cut the level of reporting, and make certain that the proper departments report to the proper people. At the same time, determine how personnel logically and effectively can be consolidated, especially in manufacturing.

Exhibit 1–1 Present Manufacturing Organization

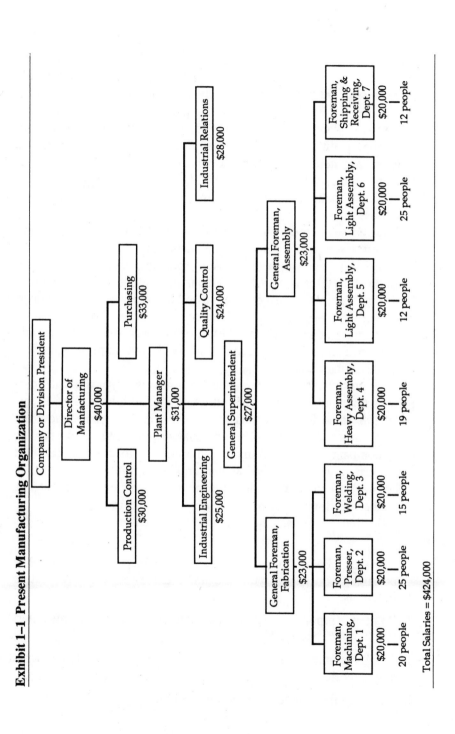

Company or Division President

Director of Manufacturing
$40,000

Production Control
$30,000

Purchasing
$33,000

Plant Manager
$31,000

Industrial Relations
$28,000

Industrial Engineering
$25,000

General Superintendent
$27,000

Quality Control
$24,000

General Foreman, Fabrication
$23,000

General Foreman, Assembly
$23,000

Foreman, Machining, Dept. 1
$20,000
20 people

Foreman, Presser, Dept. 2
$20,000
25 people

Foreman, Welding, Dept. 3
$20,000
15 people

Foreman, Heavy Assembly, Dept. 4
$20,000
19 people

Foreman, Light Assembly, Dept. 5
$20,000
12 people

Foreman, Light Assembly, Dept. 6
$20,000
25 people

Foreman, Shipping & Receiving, Dept. 7
$20,000
12 people

Total Salaries = $424,000

After studying this organizational chart you will note, for example, that there is a director of manufacturing making $40,000 to whom only three department heads report directly. One of these is the head of the purchasing department. Ask yourself if this is a good arrangement.

There is a plant manager earning $31,000, to whom the industrial engineering, quality control, and industrial relations departments report. There is a general superintendent earning $27,000, and two general foremen, one in charge of fabrication, the other in charge of assembly. They each make $23,000. Is there a way to consolidate these positions?

There are seven foremen, all of whom earn $20,000, and who are five reporting levels away from the president. One is in charge of the machine shop and supervises twenty persons; a press department foreman supervises twenty-five persons; a welding foreman employs fifteen persons; a foreman of heavy assembly supervises nineteen persons; there are two foremen of light assembly, one with twelve persons working in the department, and the other with twenty-five persons; and a foreman of shipping and receiving supervises twelve persons, including material handlers.

From those figures one can deduce that this is a typical small company or division doing from $5 million to $10 million in sales. In just about this same form, thousands of companies exist throughout the United States and in many other industrialized countries. In most cases, these companies grow and mature without ever losing their baby fat until seemingly drastic remedial measures are enforced.

Try to restructure the typical organization depicted in Exhibit 1–1 from the top down. Rediagram it on paper according to your new specifications. Approach the assignment in at least five ways:

1. Raise the reporting level of key departments to as high a level as possible, consistent with the importance of their respective functions.

2. Rearrange reporting relationships so that related departments report to the proper people.

3. Eliminate underutilized personnel and consolidate departments where feasible.

4. Minimize the number of management reporting levels.

5. Final adjustments should be made on the basis of the strengths and weaknesses of the people comprising your particular organization.

Assume that you are responsible for this organization. Allow yourself whatever time is needed to reorganize the structure. Chances are that even at first glance opportunities for immediate improvements will be apparent. Can you streamline operations, eliminating or consolidating employee positions? Are any departments reporting to the wrong people? Can any of the manufacturing departments be consolidated?

After you have tried your own skills at streamlining the organization, estimate how much you have saved in salaries and fringes. What percentage is this of a $5, $10, or $15 million dollar operation?

Exhibit 1–2 offers one way an effective reorganization could be accomplished. Bear in mind that in cost reduction (or profit improvement) there is no single answer to any given problem. If you didn't come up with the same reorganization plan as the one outlined in Exhibit 1–2, yours is not necessarily wrong, only different. Remember, always adjust your organization plan to your people and their abilities. Do not try to fit a square peg into a round hole.

You will note that by eliminating the director of manufacturing ($40,000 a year) an entire bureaucratic level has been eliminated. The reorganization has also eliminated two general foremen for a saving of $46,000 a year, and one foreman (light assembly) for an additional saving of $20,000. Retained are the plant manager and the general superintendent. Also intact are the machine shop, press, welding, and heavy assembly departments. But the two light assembly departments have been combined.

In the old organization (Exhibit 1–1), only four people reported directly to the president. This immediately violated our first rule, span of control, and also unnecessarily removed the chief executive from some of the key elements of the organization. In addition, there were simply too many levels for the chief executive to get a good feel for the strengths and weaknesses of the total manufacturing organization. In the revised organization (Exhibit 1–2), therefore, the president is two levels closer to the manufacturing departments. The president could even supervise three or four more areas if the size or nature of this particular business demanded it. For example, quality control could report directly to the president if it was a particularly important department or if it was compromised by reporting to the plant manager.

Exhibit 1-2 Revised Manufacturing Organization

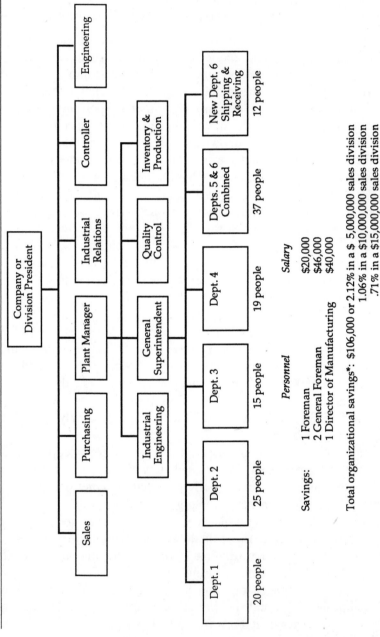

Personnel	Salary
1 Foreman	$20,000
2 General Foreman	$46,000
1 Director of Manufacturing	$40,000

Total organizational savings*: $106,000 or 2.12% in a $ 5,000,000 sales division
1.06% in a $10,000,000 sales division
.71% in a $15,000,000 sales division

*This does not even include an additional 40% which would be saved in fringes.

Under the revised plan, the plant manager will have direct responsibility for the general superintendent, industrial engineering, quality control, and inventory and production control. This still gives the plant manager the opportunity to fulfill other tasks, which is why some people would say the plant manager should also handle purchasing. But, as we already have noted, purchasing is generally where the bulk of the company's money lies, and the purchasing head should always report directly to the division president when material represents a large percentage of the sales dollar.

I could now make a case that the plant manager should be eliminated, which would allow the next level to report directly to the president. The president's span of control would then be nine, still within our range. The same argument could be made for eliminating the general superintendent but keeping the plant manager. Either change would be dramatic, however. In my judgment, we have done enough for the first year. I would allow our other changes time to settle in, and perhaps consider further changes during the next organizational analysis a year later.

Note that in the original organizational structure there was no category for inventory control, a most essential function, without which cost control cannot be practiced. We have created a department for inventory and production control which reports directly to the plant manager. (The head of production control reported to the director of manufacturing under the old organization.)

The general foremen for both fabrication and assembly have been eliminated, since under the old organization they were underutilized, using the span of control rule. The seven foremen under them have also been consolidated. Remember, our rule concerning span of control differentiates between the number of persons a foreman can supervise in a complicated operation (such as machining or heavy assembly) and a simple operation (light assembly). In the revised organizational chart we have therefore combined departments 5 and 6 so that one foreman supervises thirty-seven people in the light assembly operation but that the foreman in the heavy assembly operation has no more than nineteen people. Machining, which remains a separate department with twenty persons, is a skilled, or "difficult," operation.

What, then, can be the initial savings from a simple restructuring of your organizational chart at home, during one weekend?

- We saved the salary of the director of manufacturing, amounting to $40,000.

- We saved the salaries of two general foremen (fabrication and assembly), for a total of $46,000.

- We saved the salary of one foreman of light assembly, amounting to $20,000.

The total salary saving is $106,000, representing 2.12 percent of a company doing $5 million in sales, 1.06 percent of a company doing $10 million in sales, and seven-tenths of 1 percent for a $15 million company. We also saved 25 percent of the line manufacturing supervisory costs ($106,000 savings divided by total salary costs of $424,500), and that does not even include the savings to be realized in fringe benefits which can total approximately 40 percent of salary costs.

Not only have we cut costs, we also have decreased the levels of supervision, which should increase communication, productivity, and effectiveness. There should be as few levels as possible between top management and first line executives. The goal is to streamline the organization, connecting the president or general manager to all of the most important reporting departments so that these top executives are in direct control of all the key profit areas. With better control over key areas, they have more control over the total operation.

Case Study: Sales Organization

Once the technique of organizational analysis is mastered, it can be repeated for all subsidiaries, divisions, and departments. One of the more intriguing and effective areas for organizational revision is in sales, which surely is an area that occupies a great deal of time and thinking on the part of chief executive officers, even when they are not aggressively seeking cost reduction.

Direct your attention to Exhibit 1–3, which outlines the sales organization of our hypothetical but typical company. You will note that this selling organization has three top executives: a general sales manager, an Eastern regional sales manager, and a Western regional sales manager. Reporting to them are:

Exhibit 1–3 Present Sales Organization

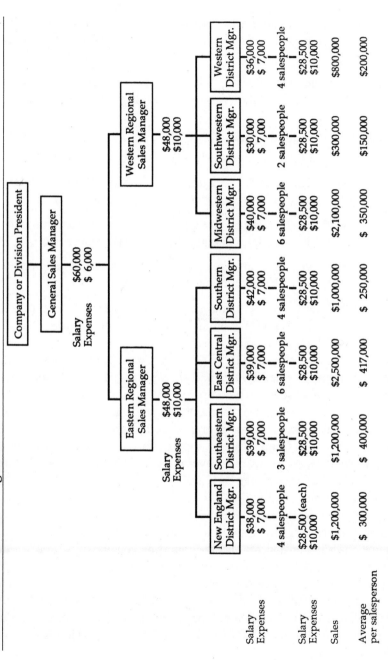

Company or Division President

General Sales Manager — Salary $60,000, Expenses $6,000

Eastern Regional Sales Manager — Salary $48,000, Expenses $10,000

Western Regional Sales Manager — Salary $48,000, Expenses $10,000

	New England District Mgr.	Southeastern District Mgr.	East Central District Mgr.	Southern District Mgr.	Midwestern District Mgr.	Southwestern District Mgr.	Western District Mgr.
Salary Expenses	$38,000 $ 7,000	$39,000 $ 7,000	$39,000 $ 7,000	$42,000 $ 7,000	$40,000 $ 7,000	$30,000 $ 7,000	$36,000 $ 7,000
	4 salespeople	3 salespeople	6 salespeople	4 salespeople	6 salespeople	2 salespeople	4 salespeople
Salary Expenses	$28,500 (each) $10,000	$28,500 $10,000	$28,500 $10,000	$28,500 $10,000	$28,500 $10,000	$28,500 $10,000	$28,500 $10,000
Sales	$1,200,000	$1,200,000	$2,500,000	$1,000,000	$2,100,000	$300,000	$800,000
Average per salesperson	$ 300,000	$ 400,000	$ 417,000	$ 250,000	$ 350,000	$150,000	$200,000

Total Salaries and Expenses = $1,611,500

- A New England district sales manager with four salespeople producing sales of $1.2 million, averaging $300,000 per salesperson.

- A Southeastern district sales manager with three salespeople producing $1.2 million in sales, averaging $400,000 per salesperson.

- An East Central district manager with six salespeople producing $2,500,000, averaging nearly $417,000 per salesperson.

- A Southern district manager, with four salespeople producing $1,000,000 in sales, averaging $250,000 per salesperson.

- A Midwestern district manager, with six salespeople producing $2.1 million in sales, averaging $350,000 per salesperson.

- A Southwestern district manager, with two salespeople producing $300,000 in sales, averaging $150,000 per salesperson.

- A Western district manager, with four salespeople producing $800,000 in sales, averaging $200,000 per salesperson.

The cast of characters: three generals, seven colonels, and twenty-nine privates, producing sales of $9.1 million. That seems like a substantial army for so small a company. Let's take a look.

At a glance you can see that there is an imbalance. Take a look at the sales per salesperson in each district. A comparison between the Southwestern and East Central district shows a serious inequity. Salespeople in the Southwestern district are averaging $150,000 apiece, while those in the East Central average $417,000, almost 300 percent greater.

Before turning to Exhibit 1–4, the revised sales organization chart, take a pencil and a piece of paper and try to work out your own reorganization as you might apply it to your own sales operation. Bear in mind the span of control and the reporting relationships that we discussed in connection with the reorganization of the manufacturing organization of this typical company. And again, don't be discouraged if your reorganization does not match the model illustrated in this text. There are no absolutes in organizational analysis or cost reduction. There are only basic rules, fundamental guidelines, and personal judgments.

Exhibit 1–4 Revised Sales Organization

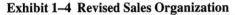

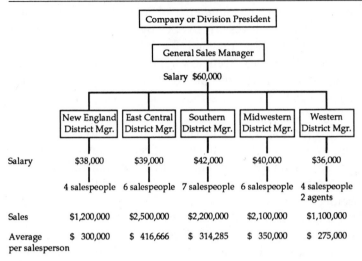

	Personnel	Salary	Expenses	
Savings:	2 Regional Managers	96,000	+ 20,000 =	116,000
	2 District Managers	69,000	+ 14,000 =	83,000
	2 Salespeople	57,000	+ 20,000 =	77,000
				276,000

Less increased costs, raises, and 2 agents
30,000 + 3,000 =   33,000

Net savings $243,000

Total organizational savings: 2.7% of this $9.1 million sales unit
15.1% of total department cost

In the revised sales organization (Exhibit 1–4) you will note that we have made some drastic changes. We have effected a thorough shake-up, simply from studying the inconsistencies and waste in the original organization.

We have eliminated the two regional managers. With seven district managers out in the field, there hardly seems to be any justification for costly regional managers. If this company is representative of a great many, the regional managers' jobs are rewards to people who have done something special for the company or who have put in many years of work, perhaps when the company was starting up or initiating growth.

We have reduced the number of district sales managers from seven to five. We have combined the Southern and Southeastern districts, and have eliminated the Southwestern district by making it part of the Western operation. The New England, East Central, and Midwestern districts have been left intact. Even now, all five district managers, and especially the individuals responsible for New England and Western districts, could actually supervise more salespeople. They therefore have room to grow.

Similarly, the general sales manager's span of control shows only five persons, which is below our stated ideal. In most companies, however, the sales manager would have other staff functions, such as inside sales, advertising, or market research, in addition to a heavy travel schedule.

All of these changes, radical though they may seem, were effected on the basis of rules concerning span of control and reporting relationships. We also took a hard look at the number of salespeople in all districts in relation to the amount of sales. It is obvious that some districts will have to be studied more closely as the cost reduction program progresses. For the time being, however, organizational analysis of the sales force is all we can accomplish during this first weekend.

Here is what the analysis achieved:

- By eliminating two regional managers, we saved $116,000 in salaries and expenses.

- By eliminating two district managers, we saved another $83,000.

- By eliminating two salespeople, we saved $77,000.

- Total salaries and expenses eliminated: $276,000.

Another 40 percent (approximately $110,400) will be saved in fringes. Although they cannot be determined precisely by this macroanalysis, neither should they be ignored or underestimated.

It will be necessary to put two new agents in the Western district at a cost of about $30,000 (a cost you pay *only* if they sell your products), and there will probably have to be raises amounting to about $3,000 to compensate for added responsibilities.

Thus the total saving will be about $276,000, minus the $33,000 for commissions and raises, for a net savings of $243,000, or 2.7 percent of the $9.1 million in sales. More significantly, this is a savings of 15.1 percent of total departmental costs ($243,000 savings divided by $1,611,500 total costs), and it does not include a probable reduction in fringes, which would result in an additional $110,400 in savings.

Remember also that with increasing energy costs and continued inflation, any travel savings made now will translate into increasingly larger savings in the future. Recent economic trends have made it prohibitive for many companies to put salespeople out on the road, and tremendously burdensome for many others. The costs of automobiles, gasoline, insurance, meals, and lodging have all skyrocketed in recent years, and in all probability will continue to do so.

It is important to note that, even with the changes we have made, sales per salesperson range between $275,000 and $416,666. Some companies will be able to average a much greater volume per salesperson, depending primarily on the profitability of the company, the product line, compound growth targets, and other particulars of the company in question. In other words, as with most of the examples throughout this text, we selected the suit of clothes from the rack, but just how you tailor the suit to your needs depends on your own particular circumstances.

Summary

At this point, based on a company with $9.1 million in sales, we have saved 1.2 percent ($106,000) by reorganizing the manufacturing department, and 2.7 percent ($243,000) by reorganizing the sales department—*for a total of 3.9 percent* (plus fringes and travel expenses). And all this can be accomplished at home, during the first weekend after deciding to undertake a cost reduction plan.

As chief executive, you should already know your own organizational structure, both in the shop and in sales. Salaries, travel expenses, and fringes can be furnished by accounting personnel. You can do the restructuring on a yellow pad while you relax with a cup of coffee. This same reorganization that you conducted for manufacturing and sales can also be applied successfully elsewhere. Any area where you have supervisory personnel and pools of employees represents an opportunity to review and reduce costs.

In summary, shoot for a savings of at least 1 to 2 percent of sales through reorganization. If you get more, you're fortunate; if you get less, question your techniques. Now you can go to work on Monday morning knowing that the first phase of the "quick and dirty" thirty-day introduction to cost reduction and its resulting profit improvement has been completed and is ready for implementation.

We have just witnessed how organizational analysis can affect immediate and substantial savings. Once you move below the supervisory level, however, it is difficult to pick up savings easily through reorganization. There are too many employees to consider. For this reason, the techniques of ratio analysis and work sampling are used to eliminate personnel excess in an industrial operation.

For example, I was once charged with reducing costs for an eastern manufacturing company which included a foundry. Through ratio analysis we discovered eleven pattern makers where there had been only three a few years earlier. A quick consultation with the foundry owner determined that the company's size and work load had not appreciably increased, and eight pattern makers were furloughed immediately. This kind of "personnel creep" can occur at any level of an organization.

Organizational analysis is used for supervisory levels. Below that, a second technique is adopted—ratio analysis.

2

The First Week—
Ratio Analysis

Following the first weekend's work on organizational analysis, the next step in the thirty-day "quick and dirty" program of cost reduction is to perform a ratio analysis of your total operation.

To do this, you will need some figures. Request from your controller the detailed department figures of the company's operations for the most recent five-year period (ten years is preferable). These are simply the fundamentals—sales, burden, gross profit, selling expenses, general and administrative costs, research and development expenditures, cost of debt service, and pretax profit—for each of the last five or ten years. For each figure you also will need its percentage in relation to sales.

If your company is less than five years old, you should use the figures for as many years as the company has been in existence. If for some other reason data is unavailable, assemble as many of the figures for as many years as possible. But most important, get your analysis underway immediately. This is what you want from your controller:

- Sales for each of the last five years.

- Material, labor, and factory burden costs for the previous five years and the percentage of sales of each.

- Gross profit for each of the last five years and each year's total as a percentage of sales.

- Selling costs for each of the last five years and each year's total as a percentage of sales.

- General and administrative (G & A) costs for the last five years and each year's total as a percentage of sales.

- Research and development (R & D) expenditures for the last five years and each year's total as a percentage of sales.

- Debt service costs for each of the last five years and each year's total as a percentage of sales.

- Figures for pretax profit for each of the last five years, with each year's total also expressed as a percentage of sales.

Macroanalysis

In assembling these figures, your purpose is to determine the lowest ratio of cost as a percentage of sales for each of these operational categories. In which year did the expenditures in each category impose the least drain on gross and/or net income?

I call this first step a macroanalysis of the figures supplied for each category as a means of setting your goals and determining minimum targets. Initially, it measures gross profit, selling costs, G & A, R & D, and debt service against sales.

On a sheet of paper lay down the five-year figures for each category, as demonstrated in Exhibit 2–1.

Next, find and circle the year that gross profit was the highest percentage of sales, and the years that selling, G & A, R & D, and debt service were the lowest percentage of sales.

If your operation is typical you will find that the best ratios did not occur in the same year. Sales were a factor, of course, but your five-year profile will undoubtedly show that gross profits were best in one year, G & A was lowest in another, selling costs were the least percentage of sales in yet another year, and so on.

Exhibit 2–1 contains the figures for a ratio analysis using the five-year history of a typical company or division. Study Exhibit 2–1. You will note that the gross profit that was the *highest* percentage of sales (29.7 percent) was in the fifth year and that the lowest ratios to sales in the remaining categories were obtained in other years. Your assignment

Exhibit 2–1 Ratio Analysis Using a Five-Year History

	Sales $	%	Gross Profit $	%	Selling $	%	G & A $	%	R & D $	%	Debt Service $	%	Pretax Profit $	%
							($ in thousands)							
Yr. 1	23,041	...	6,462	28.0	3,369	14.6	1,212	5.3	133	.6	834	2.7	1,087	4.7
Yr. 2	27,923	...	7,700	27.6	3,815	(13.7)	1,095	3.9	182	.7	720	(2.6)	1,803	6.5
Yr. 3	31,782	...	9,213	29.0	4,539	14.3	1,031	3.2	143	(.4)	995	3.2	2,504	7.7
Yr. 4	35,244	...	9,675	27.5	5,162	14.6	990	(2.8)	196	.6	1,249	3.6	2,035	5.5
Yr. 5	(37,000)	...	10,975	(29.7)	5,347	14.5	1,069	2.9	214	.6	1,122	3.0	3,250	(8.8)

Profit Attainable Using Lowest Ratio

	Sales $	%	Gross Profit $	%	Selling $	%	G & A $	%	R & D $	%	Debt Service $	%	Pretax Profit $	%
	37,000	...	10,975	29.7	5,069	13.7	1,036	2.8	148	.4	962	2.6	3,760	10.16

is to determine the profit that would be attainable by using the most favorable ratios during each of the five years of operations.

Locate the year with the highest ratio for gross profit and the years with the lowest ratios for selling, G & A, R & D, and debt service. These have been circled on the exhibit. Note that the most favorable ratios have been brought down to the bottom line. Sales will be $37,000,000, the figure for the fifth year. The other most favorable ratios are: gross profit, 29.7 percent; selling costs, 13.7 percent; general and administrative expenses, 2.8 percent; research and development, 0.4 percent; and debt service, 2.6 percent. In an ideal year, therefore, sales would have been $37,000,000, gross profit $10,975,000, selling costs $5,069,000, G & A $1,036,000, R & D outlays $148,000, and debt service $962,000. These total operating costs (they amount to $7,215,000) when subtracted from gross profit would have yielded a pretax profit of $3,760,000. Simple arithmetic allows you to discover that pretax profit has been improved by 15.7 percent (3,760/3,250) to a level of 10.16 percent on sales.

Using the best of all these ratios during the entire five-year period obviously results in a pretax profit that exceeds anything else during that period. A glance at the ratio analysis shows that pretax profits ranged from a low of 4.7 percent to a high of 8.8 percent.

One lesson to be learned from this is that there is no room for complacency. In the last of the five years under study, sales were at a peak, gross profit was at its highest level, and the pretax profit was the best for the entire period. Yet simple macro ratio analysis has shown you how the pretax profit conceivably could have been improved by more than 15 percent!

Now add the costs of material, labor, and factory burden to a chart such as the one presented in Exhibit 2–1. Again determine in which year you achieved the lowest material costs, the lowest factory burden costs, and the lowest direct labor costs. You will probably show a potential savings of another 15 percent or more. Again you will find that the lowest percentages of these three probably did not occur in the same year. Also carefully observe the trend, if there is one, in material costs. We will have more to say about this later.

Comparing Your Company with Others

After conducting a macro ratio analysis of your own company, compare your bottom line figures with those of other companies in the same industry and in the same sales bracket. These average figures can be found in the Dun & Bradstreet Reports and in the S.I.C. (Standard Industrial Classification) reports of Robert Morris Associates. If possible, obtain the 10K files and the annual reports of publicly held companies that are in your S.I.C. category and enjoy about the same amount of sales. In this way you can determine how the best performance in each category in your company's operations compares with the average performance for each category at the other companies in your industry doing about the same volume of business.

Areas of poor performance will reveal themselves immediately, and you therefore will know where to focus your attention. Remember that by this simple process of ratio analysis for one typical company—an actual case study—we were able to show how the highest pretax profit for a five-year period could be increased from 8.8 percent of sales to 10.16 percent of sales. The stark figures reveal dramatically why this function is an imperative part of your cost reduction program.

You now have completed your *macro*—broad scale—analysis. From this exercise you have determined that you have an attainable goal—*a pretax profit of 10 percent or better.*

In looking back over the five-year set of figures, the executive of the company or division might wonder what was done right in the year when costs were down to 13.7 percent of sales, or what went wrong in other years, but that is not the point of the analysis. You don't really yet have in front of you the detailed micro information necessary to make this kind of assessment. Rather, the purpose of the study was to determine what could be accomplished—to set a goal.

Microanalysis

As a next step, it is *vitally* important to determine which costs have remained in line and which have been increasing unnecessarily as a percentage of sales. This can only be accomplished through a more detailed, in-depth probe, through what we may call a microanalysis. With microanalysis you will be able to raise your target even higher.

The ratio macroanalysis you have already completed was intended to provide you with an accurate perspective (on a five- or ten-year or longer basis) on the total operations of a company or division. The next step, microanalysis, will reward you with the specifics (also culled from a five- or ten-year base) for each separate category, sharpening your focus to a point where you can readily determine the cost-cutting measures that will benefit your operations the most. This is especially true when the results of macroanalysis are compared with figures from Dun & Bradstreet and the S.I.C.'s, and with the annual reports or 10Ks of other companies when available.

Under organizational analysis, the sales department of our prototypic company came in for some serious reorganization (see Chapter 1). In this chapter, macroanalysis has demonstrated that selling costs have been mounting steadily, and that as a percentage of sales they average about 14.5 percent with, of course, the one exception that was noted in the analysis.

Ordinarily you would conduct your microanalysis, as well as all cost reduction efforts, in the order of categories involving the most dollars. You should observe a system of priorities (in Chapters 4 and 5 we discuss these priorities at greater length). We have already mentioned, for example, the purchasing department's effect on profits, and three entire chapters in Part III of this text are devoted to cutting material costs.

For the purpose of this example, however, let us continue to concentrate on sales, and proceed with a microanalysis of marketing for this same company. Recall that the macroanalysis revealed that in the most favorable year, selling costs were 13.7 percent of total sales (actually it was 13.67 percent, rounded to 13.7 percent).

The same numbers that were required for macroanalysis are now needed for micro. In this example, you also would ask your controller for a breakdown of the selling costs for the last five (or ten) years so that you can look at them on a lowest cost basis, just as you did for general operations. Exhibit 2–2 breaks down selling costs for a typical company, although the specific categories for your own company might vary. Depending on the nature of your business, for example, you also may want to itemize commissions, advertising, telephone, warehouse rent and taxes, office supplies, postage, depreciation, and insurance.

By circling the lowest ratio in each category or function of the selling operations, we have done part of your assignment for you. We have determined the lowest cost in that particular activity in relation to net sales.

Check this work on the exhibit carefully. Note that salaries and wages in the home office had their lowest ratio to net sales in year 3 at 1.53 percent. The other most favorable ratios are:

- Fringe benefits, .08 percent.
- Travel and expenses, .37 percent.
- Sales meetings and conventions, .23 percent.
- Other expenses and costs, .69 percent

For branch office costs, the best ratios were:

- Supervisors, .51 percent.
- Salespeople's salaries and commissions, 2.18 percent.
- Stockhandlers, .80 percent.

Exhibit 2–2 Ratio Analysis in the Selling Expense Area

	Year 1 $	Year 1 % to NS	Year 2 $	Year 2 % to NS	Year 3 $	Year 3 % to NS	Year 4 $	Year 4 % to NS	Year 5 $	Year 5 % to NS	Lowest Cost/Ratio $	Lowest Cost/Ratio % to NS
Net Sales (NS)	23,041,000	100.00	27,872,000	100.00	31,782,000	100.00	35,244,000	100.00	37,000,000	100.00		
Selling Home Office												
Salaries, Wages, etc.	471,002	2.04	478,864	1.72	486,745	1.53	649,821	1.84	753,962	2.04		1.53
Fringe Benefits	19,102	.08	32,470	.12	53,043	.17	64,025	.18	94,861	.26		.08
Travel and Entertainment	84,291	.37	102,785	.37	43,002	.45	157,469	.45	155,820	.42		.37
Sales Meetings and Conventions	54,009	.23	80,967	.29	82,233	.26	93,182	.27	103,842	.28		.23
Other	208,853	.91	193,291	.69	248,186	.78	394,928	1.12	388,386	1.05		.69
Total	837,257	3.63	888,377	3.19	1,013,249	3.19	1,359,425	3.86	1,498,872	4.05	1,073,000	2.90
Branch Expense												
Supervisors	136,784	.59	141,120	.51	175,043	.55	202,489	.57	215,567	.58		.51
Salespeople's Salaries and Commissions	566,434	2.46	647,788	2.32	706,897	2.23	782,903	2.22	805,891	2.18		2.18
Stockhandlers	184,271	.80	235,768	.84	296,977	.93	353,784	1.00	311,972	.85		.80
Other Wages	109,398	.48	110,708	.40	149,904	.47	159,571	.45	115,478	.31		.31
Fringe Benefits	63,129	.27	108,988	.38	144,249	.45	179,938	.51	190,587	.52		.27
Fixed Expenses	299,510	1.30	361,273	1.30	398,387	1.25	386,133	1.10	444,061	1.20		1.10
Travel and Entertainment	184,916	.80	197,473	.71	215,184	.68	215,414	.61	266,360	.72		.61
Freight (all-inclusive)	184,430	.80	229,265	.82	297,666	.94	301,651	.86	278,000	.75		.75
Other	181,622	.79	186,454	.67	244,669	.77	249,346	.71	234,090	.63		.63
Total	1,910,494	8.29	2,216,837	7.95	2,628,976	8.27	2,831,229	8.03	2,862,004	7.74	2,649,200	7.16
Outlying Plants	20,627	.09	21,439	.08	24,862	.08	34,712	.10	31,152	.08	31,152	.08
Advertising	600,220	2.61	682,150	2.45	849,493	2.67	936,295	2.65	900,000	2.43	900,000	2.43
Grand Total	3,368,598	14.62	3,808,803	13.67	4,538,874	14.28	5,161,861	14.64	5,348,849	14.45	4,653,350	12.57
Potential Savings											693,299	
Number of Ratios Used		5		3⅓		1⅓		2		5⅓		1.32

- Other wages, .31 percent.
- Fringe benefits, .27 percent.
- Fixed expenses, 1.10 percent.
- Travel and entertainment, .61 percent.
- Freight, .75 percent.
- Other expenses, .63 percent.
- Outlying plants, tied for three years at.08 percent.
- Advertising, 2.43 percent.

In Exhibit 2–2 all these figures have been brought down in order to come up with a ratio of total selling costs to total sales. As we demonstrated with macroanalysis, the most favorable ratio is 13.67 percent.

If you will check the circled figures once more, you will see that this company had five of its best ratios in the first year, three and one-third in the second year, one and one-third in the third year, and five and one-third in the fifth. If you apply these most favorable ratios to each category—as illustrated on the extreme right of the exhibit—you will find that your selling costs amount to $4,653,350, or 12.57 percent of the highest net sales of $37,000,000.

You will recall that on the macrochart the most favorable ratio was 13.67 percent. By applying *microanalysis* you might possibly pull it down by 1.10 percentage points to 12.57, which in this case amounts to $693,299.

Looking critically at the chart, you will detect that fringe benefits established their lowest ratios in the most distant year, and your reaction to this, quite naturally, might be to decide that fringe benefits are difficult to cut; they tend to increase in our present society. This is true, of course, but fringes can be considered in tandem with wages and salaries. They are both a function of personnel, and the elimination of unnecessary or underutilized personnel will result in lower overall costs. A further advantage of this microanalysis, therefore, is that such a breakdown permits you to visualize the insidious creep of so-called fringe benefits.

Looking at the total picture, macro- and microanalyses have revealed a potential savings of nearly $700,000 annually in this company's sales department alone. In a company that makes 5 percent pretax profit, an additional $14,000,000 in sales ($700,000 ÷ 0.05) would be needed to match this bottom line result; in a company that makes a 10 percent pretax profit, it is the equivalent of $7,000,000 ($700,000 ÷ 0.10) in additional sales.

One of this book's most important messages is that this $700,000 in added profit is of much greater benefit to a company than a comparable increase in sales. It is vital to keep in mind that cost reduction can be realized without the necessity of generating and paying for additional working capital, which can run into many millions of dollars in added inventory, obsolescence, accounts receivable, reserves, and interest charges. Additional plant and equipment also might be necessary to increase sales. Particularly during periods of high interest rates, increased debt (which usually accompanies increased sales) can totally nullify your sales gain and actually put you in a loss position. That's why cost reduction techniques are so effective; you don't have to create new working capital, debt, interest charges, new inexperienced labor, and burden to obtain added profits. (Exhibits 4–3 and 4–4 and the accompanying discussion in Chapter 4 will clearly demonstrate the implications and potential dangers of increasing sales without also focusing on cost reduction measures.)

But for now, the most important point to remember about cost reduction—and this will be stressed over and over again—is that the best way to increase profit is not to increase sales, but to cut costs. When costs are cut there is no need to bring in new debt money for increased working capital in the form of accounts receivable or inventory.

Axiom: Sales cost money; cost reduction costs nothing.

Analyzing All Departmental Areas

Let us take a moment and summarize the potential substantial savings we have realized through the limited ratio analysis conducted in this chapter:

- Through macroanalysis we can raise pretax profit from 8.8 percent to 10.16, for a savings of 1.36 percent (see Exhibit 2–1).

- As part of macroanalysis in one category only (sales) we can cut expenses from 14.5 to 13.7, for a potential savings of .8 percent (see Exhibit 2–1).

- Your sales expense reduction potential through microanalysis is from 13.67 percent (Year 2) to 12.57 percent, for a potential savings of 1.10 percent (see Exhibit 2–2).

And remember, in order to improve your return on sales by another several percentage points, a microanalysis also can be applied to factory burden, G & A, and various other areas. It can even be applied to a department such as purchasing. Although the cost of materials and direct labor do not lend themselves to these methods, all other purchasing costs, such as personnel and overhead, can be broken down in order to pinpoint areas of potential cost reduction.

Ratio analysis certainly should be applied to burden, which can make up more than 20 percent of all costs, as will be demonstrated in later chapters. In Exhibit 2–3, the burden costs of another typical manufacturing company have been broken down. Again, the lowest percentage for each item should be circled. Analyses for each area can then be conducted, similar to the one conducted for sales in Exhibit 2–2.

In Exhibit 2–3, notice the steady upward creep of the overall burden percentage. What should your target be for Year 6? Where can the greatest savings be realized? Begin as we did in the other exhibits in this chapter by circling the lowest figure in each category. One of the first problem areas you should notice is that the cost of indirect labor has skyrocketed at a greater rate than most other items. There is an opportunity here for cost reduction, a conclusion which can be verified by using a constant dollar chart as described in the next section.

Constant Dollar per Employee

There is another very simple yet extremely useful and effective method to measure the health of a company. It should be conducted at the same time as ratio analysis and, like ratio analysis, it can provide you at a glance with some very valuable information about your company and/or division.

Exhibit 2-3 Microanalysis of Burden Costs

(% of Sales Dollar)

Burden Expenses	Year 1	Year 2	Year 3	Year 4	Year 5
Salaries	3.5	3.2	3.5	3.6	3.6
Benefits	.6	.4	.7	.8	1.0
Indirect Labor	3.7	4.1	5.1	5.6	5.9
Hourly Benefits	2.2	3.2	3.1	3.8	3.6
Supplies	1.2	1.4	1.2	1.2	1.2
Maintaining Parts/Tools	.9	1.2	.8	.9	1.0
Utilities	.6	.8	.6	.8	.7
Depreciations	1.2	2.5	1.8	1.6	1.6
Taxes	.5	.7	.5	.5	.5
Insurance	.2	.2	.3	.3	.4
Leased Building	1.4	1.1	1.2	1.2	.9
Equipment Rental	.1	.2	.1	.2	.2
Miscellaneous	.5	.3	.5	.8	.7
Transfer Out	(.3)	(.1)	(.4)	(.1)	(.2)
Total	16.3	19.2	19.0	21.2	21.1

Often a company or division president will use an increase in sales per employee as evidence of the organization's increased productivity and earnings. Unless the figures are adjusted for inflation, however, such an analysis can be misleading. On the other hand, a constant dollar method can be an invaluable tool. In fact, a chart mapping the annual constant dollar sales per employee is often the first piece of information that should be inspected when division or department heads present their annual review to top executives. This graph can instantly demonstrate not only worker productivity, but can also suggest the status of overall management efficiency.

Study Exhibit 2–4. Immediately it can be determined that although this company has increased its sales steadily during the most recent

Exhibit 2–4 Constant Dollar Sales Versus Employee Graph

Sales per Employee (in $s)

	Year 1	Year 2	Year 3	Year 4	Year 5	Year 6
Salaried - Exempt	38	38	36	34	39	45
Salaried - Nonexempt	28	30	25	33	31	33
Hourly - Direct	77	83	79	76	96	108
Hourly - Indirect	28	37	38	51	42	42
Total Employees	171	188	178	194	208	228
OT (Overtime) Equivalents (included above)						
Salaried	0	1	1	1	1	1
Hourly	6	8	3	10	9	9
Total OT Equivalents	6	9	4	11	10	10
Net Sales (in thousands)	4,906	5,712	6,654	6,997	7,900	9,200
Constant Dollar Sales (CDS)[1] (in thousands)	8,004	8,81u	8,458	8,464	8,532	9,200
CDS/Total Employees (nearest dollar)	46,807	46,862	47,517	43,629	41,019	40,351

[1]Adjusted utilizing the consumer price index for urban users using 1974 as the base year.

five-year period—from a little less than $5 million to more than $9 million, and although the number of employees has increased by only 30 percent, the real story is told when constant dollar figures are used. Constant dollar sales per employee have actually decreased from $46,807 to $40,351. Notice that three of the four wage and salary categories appear to have increased abnormally. A quick set of ratio calculations will confirm this and provide direction for your cost reduction (see Exhibit 2-5).

Armed with the information gleaned from this graph and its numbers, the more in-depth data provided by ratio analysis can be approached with the knowledge that somewhere there probably are degenerative, although solvable, problems in this organization. More often than not, you will find that such a decline is the result of insufficient controls on personnel or material costs, a faulty pricing mechanism, or being lulled by inflated sales dollar growth. (Purchasing and pricing will both be discussed in detail in later chapters.)

By investigating Exhibit 2–4 further, you will note that the best ratio of constant dollar sales to employee was obtained in Year 3, after which this ratio dropped off rather sharply. It is useful to determine what this drop-off means in real terms. By dividing the constant dollar sales for Year 6 (9,200) by the constant dollar sales for Year 3 (8,458), you will note that, after adjusting for inflation, sales have had a real growth of 9 percent (9200 ÷ 8458 = 1.0877, rounded to 1.09). The number of

Exhibit 2–5 Documentation of Personnel Creep from Constant Dollar Graph

	Year 3	Year 6 Target	Year 6 Actual	Difference between Target and Actual
Salaried—Exempt	36 x 1.09 =	39	45	6
Salaried—Nonexempt	25 x 1.09 =	27	33	6
Hourly—Direct	79 x 1.09 =	86	108	22
Hourly—Indirect	38 x 1.09 =	41	42	1
Total Employees	178	193	228	35

employees, therefore, should not have increased by more than 9 percent. Note that:

- Salaried exempt employees should have numbered 39 rather than 45.

- Salaried nonexempt employees should have numbered 27 rather than 33.

- Hourly direct employees should have numbered 86 rather than 108.

- Hourly indirect employees should have numbered 41 rather than 42.

This company, therefore, has approximately thirty-five too many employees. By adding workers according to the actual sales dollars rather than constant dollars, this company ended up with an unnecessary employee surplus of almost 19 percent! Remember, this assumes that in Year 3 the four categories of personnel were fully efficient. There actually is no reason to make this assumption. In fact, to the extent the company was inefficient in Year 3, the problem of excess costs due to excess personnel is further compounded.

It should be noted that, depending on a variety of factors—including type of business—companies will vary widely as to their sales per employee. The company charted in Exhibit 2–4 happens to have between $40,000 and $50,000 in sales per employee, but I've been involved with companies that are getting over $100,000 in constant dollar sales. Regardless of where a company falls in the spectrum, the goal should be to increase the ratio of constant dollars per employee.

Summary

At this stage we are one week into the "quick and dirty" cost reduction program. By obtaining fairly detailed departmental budget figures from your controller you have pinpointed specific targeted goals.

A word of caution at this point. You will be surprised to observe how many changes in accounting procedures may have taken place over a ten-year, or even a five-year, period. All sorts of reasons and excuses will be forthcoming.

This will provide you with an excellent chance to see how good your accounting and control really is. By becoming familiar with your controller's techniques and methods, you will make certain that your company's accounting procedures become standardized, comprehensive, up-to-date, and readily accessible. The happy results: First, your controller will keep you better informed of internal techniques in future years. Second, you will have a much better appraisal and understanding of your controller and your accounting procedures.

Next will be the third and final phase of the "quick and dirty" introduction to cost reduction. Phase 3 is a work sampling analysis. It can be accomplished during the balance of the month—about another three or four weeks—and will require the assistance of your industrial engineer and quite possibly an outside industrial engineering consultant.

3

The First Month—
Work Sampling

At this point you have taken four essential introductory steps:

Area   I: Organizational Analysis

   1. During the first weekend you have completed your organizational analysis.

Area II: Ratio Analysis

   2. During the following week you have completed a macroanalysis of your company and microanalyses of labor, burden, selling, general administrative, research and development costs (if any), and determined any changes in your material percentage.

   3. You have looked at your constant dollar chart and its supporting data to see the trend in sales per employee adjusted for inflation; and the variations and trends in your four employee categories of salaried exempt, salaried nonexempt, and direct and indirect labor.

   4. Also during the first week you have compared your analyses with the representative figures presented by both Dun & Bradstreet and Robert Morris Associates, and, where available, with your competitor's annual reports and 10Ks and any other relative comparative data.

The remainder of the time in this month-long "quick and dirty" program of cost reduction will be spent on work sampling. Reduced to its simplest form, work sampling is a random sampling method for obtaining facts about human activities and machines by the application of observation and mathematical probabilities. It is a useful, yet grossly underutilized tool of management. By sampling the frequency and effectiveness of activity at the various work stations within a plant or an office, work sampling can pinpoint specific areas of both worker and/or machine productivity and inefficiency levels.

Work sampling is one of the most effective, practical, and scientific approaches to cost reduction, and is the best tool for intelligently and quickly eliminating unnecessary personnel. It is also relatively inexpensive and avoids costly errors. It can further serve as a substitute for work standards or provide a general appraisal of your existing standards system and equipment utilization (see Chapter 11).

Work sampling begins with a work sampling observer going into a given area of a shop or office to observe specified functions. The observer records what everyone is doing, the pace at which they are doing it, and what is happening at each machine or function. These observations are made hundreds of times, at random, with absolutely no set time schedules.

There are some who refer to work sampling as "ratio delay studies," but it should be noted that this term is no longer in vogue for two practical reasons. The first is obvious: We are not really looking for delays, but for enhancement in production. Second, we are observing and "sampling" work, not idleness. Some industrial engineers use the acceptable term "observation ratios," which is just about as accurate a description as "work sampling." However, "work sampling" is more acceptable psychologically to the average employee, and since employees usually are aware of management efforts to increase productivity, and often discuss these efforts among themselves, work sampling seems to be the more appropriate description.

Before undertaking a work sampling operation, it is vital to make the job as direct and uncomplicated as possible. Remember, work sampling is simply a method of making random observations for determining the relationship of delays and the elements of work to the total time it takes to process an item. With these random observations you are seeking to learn the time the operator and/or machine spends in setup, operation, maintenance, delay, or at rest, as well as the work pace of the operator.

A work sampling operation should be instigated by either an internal employee experienced in work sampling, probably an industrial engineer, or by an outside consultant competent in this area. While you should have such expert guidance, you would be equally well-advised to have at least a general understanding of the logic behind the work sampling process.

In order to complete a work sampling procedure within the initial thirty-day period, the process should be begun immediately. In fact, on the Monday after the weekend spent conducting an organizational analysis, you should sit down with the work sampling expert and discuss a procedure and timetable. It will take at least a week for the professional in charge of your work sampling to acquire the necessary employee and machinery data, as well as to explain the procedure to all appropriate employees. This will leave about three weeks for the actual work sampling operation, which can be conducted concurrently with your own implementation of reorganization and ratio analysis.

Work sampling, while costing a small fraction of a regular continuous standards program, will provide invaluable information concerning three vital aspects of an operation:

1. Percentage of time employees are working.

2. Rate at which employees are working.

3. Utilization of machinery.

In other words, work sampling will provide a reliable estimate of the efficiency of your shop and/or office and the utilization levels of your various pieces of equipment.

The Procedure

It takes only about a day to teach someone how to be an observer in a work sampling study, provided the observers are supervised by a competent industrial engineer. Ideally, one day should be devoted to having the industrial engineer or outside consultant train the observers, another day to designing the study and setting up the program, and two days for dry runs before starting to compile results.

The executive in charge of the work sampling should arrange a brief meeting with all department supervisors before beginning the observation phase. The theory and purpose of work sampling should be explained. Supervisors will also be asked to provide all available attendance and production records for their departments.

Next, observers must be chosen. As a rule of thumb, one observer will be needed for every eighty to one hundred employees. Regular employees can be used for this task, or hourly workers, even high school students. There are, however, a number of important factors involved in good work sampling. Observers should have or acquire at least a general knowledge of the operations in question. Observers should be given maps of the sampling areas so that they know precisely what areas they are required to cover. The observers should be available 100 percent of the time during sampling. And probably most important, *employees should never sample their own departments.*

Probability Theory

Work sampling is based on observations made long ago—certainly as far back as the Roman Empire, probably earlier—while flipping coins. The basic law is this: If you flip a coin long enough it will tend to come up heads half the time (50 percent) and tails half the time (50 percent).

The key, however, is to determine how many flips are necessary in order to obtain accurate results within an acceptable margin of error. Two flips of a coin, for example, obviously would be inadequate. The coin could too easily come up heads twice or tails twice rather than obey the laws of probability by coming up heads once and tails once. Even ten flips may not be enough. But a coin flipped one hundred times will come very close to coming up heads fifty times and tails fifty times. Try it. You can be sure that a coin flipped 1,000 times will come even closer, on a percentage basis, to 50 percent heads and 50 percent tails. The more flips, the greater the statistical reliability.

This is the *law of probability,* applied most effectively in the gaming halls of Las Vegas and Monte Carlo, in scientific laboratories, and in statistical mathematical projections, as well as in the modern manufacturing plant. Statistical quality control tends to be based on this same theory. Its accuracy can be controlled, for it depends on the percentage of occurrence and the frequency of observation.

Perhaps the most important thing to remember about work sampling is that *due to the law of probability, the greater the number of observations that you make, the more accurate will be your study*. It is also important to remember that while workers may speed up temporarily and distort early observations, they will soon return to their normal pattern, so any bias is short-lived and easily identifiable.

Your industrial engineer or management consultant will help you in determining how to set up the required frequencies of observation for any given function. They will help you set up nomographs, having decided in advance how frequently something will be observed. Numerous industrial engineering manuals list tables illustrating the mathematics of work sampling. They have been carefully prepared by experts so that they have acceptable built-in tolerances. An example of such a nomograph, as well as a corresponding explanation, appears in Appendix I in the back of this book.

Having been informed as to how many observations must be made in a specified period of time, the observer sets up a timetable to make certain that the observations will be made strictly at random and in the prescribed number each day. The assignment: to record exactly what is happening with the machine and its operator at the precise instant it is observed. If it is determined, for example, that 590 observations must be made in 30 working days, the observer will know to make 20 observations per day for 20 days and 19 observations per day for the remaining 10 days.

These observations should be made at varying times, and *never at the same time each day*. An essential requirement of a good work sampling is that the tours be taken at random intervals so that any given instant has as much chance of being selected as any other. This is accomplished through the use of a random number table such as the one in Exhibit A–2, to be found in Appendix I, which has been prepared to provide a more technical insight into work sampling. Remember, work sampling should be organized and directed by a trained practitioner.

A Method for All Types of Shops

Although work sampling is used primarily in nonincentive shops, it can also be used in an incentive shop as a valuable method to determine whether or not an incentive program's standards are too loose. A work sampling program might find, for example, that a shop that is being paid for 110 percent efficiency is actually working at only 80 percent efficiency. ,

Work sampling should be utilized no matter what kind of standards program has been established. Some manufacturing operations use historical standards; others use time studies, which are simply stopwatch methods of breaking down jobs into their various elements; and still others use the much more accurate methods time measurement (MTM) or its offshoots, which break down a job into much smaller components of micromotions. MTM is a particularly valuable tool because it allows an estimate to be made for cost and even pricing purposes, creating the standard for a job before it ever reaches the floor. Improvements derived from new techniques or methods can thus easily be translated into revised standards. A more detailed discussion of the different kinds of standards programs appears in Chapter 11.

Regardless of the standards program in place in your particular company—historical standards, time studies, MTM, incentive or nonincentive—work sampling is an invaluable tool for quickly, inexpensively, and effectively providing a clear reading of productivity in any given office, plant, or specific task. It is much less expensive than any continuous standards program, and it will not be skewed by misleading temporary fluctuations in efficiency or by operational improvements. Not only does it show where direct labor costs can be quickly eliminated, it also identifies areas where costs can be eliminated or reduced in both indirect labor and office operations, which normally are difficult to control.

Attendance Records

It is absolutely essential that the department head whose machinery and functions are being observed keep accurate attendance records. Unreported or unrecorded absenteeism can wreak havoc on your calculations. If an employee is temporarily absent from the department, the observer must note this in the records; otherwise, the percentage figures showing efficiency will be inaccurate. Absenteeism, in fact, can play an important role in your ultimate decision concerning the necessary number of employees within a particular department.

For example, if the work sampling study shows that a department of fifty employees could be reduced by 10 percent, or five people, and you know that the department has a consistent record of 10 percent absenteeism, you can require that the department head lay off six people (the five plus one). This would also mean, of course, that you'd better take a good, hard look at your absentee problem.

Thus, if the rate of absenteeism is not known, total efficiency cannot be achieved. Therefore, the first notation made by the work sampling observers should be the number of employees in the department or operation in question. The reasons for discrepancies between the number of employees who are supposed to be working in the observed operation and the number of employees actually working should be noted using a code similar to the one in Exhibit A–7 in Appendix I.

Productive and Nonproductive Factory and Office Work

Definitions also can be found in Appendix I for recording the productive and nonproductive status of all workers both in a manufacturing operation and in an office. These two terms are largely self-explanatory. Productive time is time spent productively. Nonproductive time is time spent nonproductively.

It should be noted that by its very nature, an office situation is more difficult to work sample than a manufacturing operation. The goals and tasks of office work are more difficult to determine precisely. Nevertheless, work sampling an office situation can be just as cost effective. The theory and procedures are certainly the same. Only the productive and nonproductive definitions differ.

Setup Time

Setup time, the time spent by an operator setting up a machine in preparation for running it, should be treated as a third work status category to go along with productive and nonproductive. If setup is considered as productive time, a company's work sampling calculation can easily be misleadingly optimistic. If setup is considered nonproductive, the resulting calculations may be misleadingly pessimistic.

A good rule of thumb is that a piece of manufacturing machinery should have a minimum of five hours of run time for every one hour of setup. A ten-to-one ratio is, of course, even more desirable. If your ratios are lower, perhaps your products are being poorly routed or your production scheduling and/or inventory control is faulty.

Pace Rating

Pace rating is used to determine the rate at which employees are working, with 100 percent being the amount of work an average worker will accomplish maintaining an average pace within a normal eight-hour day.

The rating should be done by a trained observer. Films are available showing various operations performed at different rates to sharpen or develop pace rating skills. These films should be shown to all observers as part of their training process. Observers will determine how they rate in relation to a norm. Although some observers will rate tightly, and others more loosely, they all will tend to be consistent and therefore can be adjusted against a norm. For example, observers who are consistently 10 percent too lenient will know to adjust their rating accordingly.

The observer samples each operation and rates each worker. These rated observations are then used to determine the average pace of the group.

In summarizing the work samplings, as in setting time standards, allowances should be given. While percentages may vary from company to company, a normal average is 5 percent personal, 5 percent fatigue, and 5 percent for unavoidable delays. The 15 percent total is applied when the total work sampling data is summarized. An additional delay allowance may be required for a specific job class, and a space is supplied on the recap sheet for this purpose.

A work sampling pace rate summary chart appears as Exhibit A–13 in Appendix I.

Machine Utilization

Not only is it important to determine the productivity of workers, it is equally important to measure the utilization of machinery. The goal is the same: to determine if there is too much or too little machinery in any one area. Without work sampling, expensive machinery can remain idle or almost idle, unnecessarily tying up capital and space, thereby increasing burden.

If a machine is underutilized, it may be cost effective to contract out the job or run the jobs on other machines in order to eliminate the need for some equipment. (I once sampled a factory in which the one thousand pieces of equipment had only an 11 percent utilization. Just imagine the wasted space and underutilized capital investment.) On the other hand, if a particular machine is overutilized, a new purchase of an identical, or more efficient, piece of machinery may be in order. Sale of excess machinery can be used to offset some of the cost of new equipment.

The purpose of a machine utilization survey, therefore, is to determine the amount of time a machine is being utilized productively and the amount of time it is idle or nonproductive, and to assist management in identifying and defining potential excesses or shortages of equipment. Once the number of observations, time sequences, and sampling routes are established, the observations should be recorded using a consistent set of definitions. An example of the kind of definitions which can be used appears as Exhibit A–14 in Appendix I.

A machine utilization sampling immediately indicates areas where either too much or too little machinery is available. If, for example, the percentage of setup is high, this means that for one reason or another inefficiency has set in. A closer look at your entire work sampling operation should suggest reasons why. If, on the other hand, the percentage of setup is low but maintenance time is high, this also should be a signal that something is amiss. Perhaps a preventative maintenance program is needed, or perhaps the machinery itself is faulty or too old.

By the same token, if both maintenance time and machine tool setup are low, and your run time is in line, but your machinery is idle 50 percent of the time, then you have too much equipment, or a poor job is being done in production control, or the wrong equipment is being utilized.

Summarizing Results

After a work sampling program is completed, a final report should be written summarizing the findings and proposing suggestions that will reduce labor costs. Recommended work force reductions should be outlined in detail for each department and information about the combining of work tasks presented. Also included should be an outline of any problems that the sampling indicates a department may be having. Suggested solutions should be costed with regard to capital expenses and savings.

In order to assist in the evaluation of the work sampling operation, a summary chart such as Exhibit 3–1 can be used. After noting the department number and job class, the number of employees are calculated, taking into account the absentee rate that the work sampling has provided.

The work sampling will also generate a productive work percentage, which now should be added to a total delay allowance so that a final revised productive percentage can be determined. The total delay allowance is the percentage of time that a delay impinges on the specific job being observed. For example, for an office job in which telephoning is required, there will have to be a certain percentage of time taken into account for delays—being put on hold, wrong numbers, finding a number, talking to intermediaries, etc.

This revised productive percentage is then multiplied by the pace percentage which is an evaluation of whether the pace rate revealed by the work sampling program is below, above, or at the norm. And finally, the revised productive percentage is multiplied by a personal, fatigue and delay (PF&D) allowance of 15 percent (multiplied, therefore, by 1.15). The result of these calculations is a net performance index (NPI).

The next column in Exhibit 3–1, "Optimum Required," is simply the number of employees needed if the performance goal of 100 percent were attained. The variance is the difference between the optimum required and the actual number of employees on the job. It is attained by multiplying the NPI by the number of employees. It will indicate if, and by how many, a department could be trimmed. Note that there is a column for the maximum number of employees that can be cut, and for the recommended number. They will not always be identical.

Finally, a work sampling summary chart should always include a "Remarks" column to allow for further recommendations as to ways in which efficiency might be enhanced.

Efficiency

The goal of any work sampling study is to increase efficiency and productivity and to eliminate excess. With work sampling you can evaluate the utilization efficiency of your machinery and of your personnel. It permits you to cut your costs intelligently and to determine and maintain at least interim standards.

Exhibit 3-1 Work Sampling Summary

Division _____
Plant _____

Study Period _____
Page _____ of _____ Date _____

Dept. No.	Department Description	Job Classification	Number of Employees			Ab-sentee Rate	Raw Productive %	Total Delay Allowance	Revised Productive %	% Pace	% PF&D Allowance	Net Performance Index	Optimum Required	Variance	Excess Employees		Remarks*
			Payroll	Payroll Less Excused lv. & abs.	Study										Maximum	Recommended	

*In an actual operation this column should have sufficient room for personal comments, which sometimes can be even more important than "the facts."

Instead of telling your manufacturing head, "I have looked over our ratio analyses and constant dollar chart and they show that we can take a cut of 10 percent in the work force, so do it," by work sampling you can determine where you are overstaffed in each work center, both in production areas and in offices. Perhaps there are even places where you are understaffed. Do not be surprised to find, however, that in some areas you will be *over*staffed by 100 percent. Work sampling identifies problems with individual performance, machine utilization, tooling, quality, maintenance, and material handling. It is an extremely valuable and expeditious method for use by foremen, as well as other plant or office   management personnel, including the division or company president.

My own experience indicates that a reduction in work force averaging at least 10 percent can be made on the initial work sampling, within the first month that this phase of cost reduction is undertaken. You will also have an excellent knowledge of your machine utilization and an accurate, informed assessment of your personnel by the time your initial work sampling study has been completed. In an incentive shop it will quickly demonstrate the condition of your incentive plan versus your actual productivity.

At this point you should inaugurate a program of *continuing* work sampling. This is virtually the only way to avoid the phenomenon of having excess personnel creep back into the production shop or onto the office work force. It happens all the time. And remember, work sampling conducted on a regular basis need not be expensive. Once an effective, streamlined work sampling operation is underway, it can be conducted by unskilled (although intelligent), relatively inexpensive, but trained part-time employees—high school or college students, for example.

Summary

With the completion of your work sampling study, your "quick and dirty" program is ended. It should require about a month, possibly a bit more. With these three steps—*organizational analysis, ratio analysis, and work sampling*—you should have reduced the cost of "people" by 10 to 20 percent. This alone can increase your pretax profits by two to five percentage points, providing you ensure that these savings reach the bottom line (see Chapter 10).

Both organizational analysis and ratio analysis should be repeated at least once a year, while work sampling in most cases should be maintained on a continuing basis. One of our divisions has put its work sampling on computer, and calls out the results on a frequent and regular basis. If for some reason your company fails to establish a continuing work sampling operation, it should be repeated in total at least once a year.

The next step in your overall cost reduction effort will call for more in-depth procedures and will require the better part of a year to complete. The "q and d" measures already conducted, however, in thirty days and with very little investment should pay for these longer, more costly subsequent programs, and at the same time add substantially to pretax profits.

II

Orientation

4

Setting the Priorities

Following the launching of the thirty-day "quick and dirty" portion of your cost reduction program, it immediately should become a permanent part of your operating procedures. No matter how efficient you believe your operation to be, a continuous, persistent program of organizational analysis, ratio analysis, and work sampling should be of major concern to you. No single thirty-day program will eliminate all the inefficiencies and waste in an organization; and it certainly will not prevent the same problems from slipping back into your organization.

It is remarkable that in many if not most cases, a thirty-day cost reduction program can not only cut at least 2 to 5 percent of total sales costs the first time it is conducted, but similar savings can be accomplished year after year. And regardless of how much waste has been allowed to creep back into your organization in a year's time, you are safe in the knowledge that your "q and d" method is costing you very little, and thus is a no-risk but potentially very profitable technique which should be repeated at least once a year.

I know of one highly successful company which assigned an industrial engineer to each of its manufacturing areas with instructions to eliminate 15 percent of the costs each year. They were paid incentives on results achieved and averaged five years in each area. How would you like to be the third or fourth person going into an area knowing you were still required to get 15 percent out each year? The initial year of such a program probably wouldn't be too difficult, or even the second year. But each successive year would of course become increasingly difficult. The program, however, has been remarkably successful over a long period of time.

Cost Reduction Priorities

The next step in your total cost reduction program, after the first thirty days, is to establish your priorities. Where can the greatest savings be realized, and therefore where should you concentrate your efforts? Exhibit 4–1 is an expansion and revision of Exhibit 2–1. It divides the sales dollar into its eight major components.

Exhibit 4–1 presents a P & L breakdown for a hypothetical metal fabricating company. Your company of course will have its own breakdown, which may or may not be similar. It is astounding how many presidents cannot make a table such as this for their company from memory. If you aren't aware of where the bulk of your money is going, you can't possibly know in what areas cost reduction will have the greatest impact.

Exhibit 4–1 Profit and Loss Breakdown Analysis of Typical Manufacturing Company

Material	45%
Direct Labor	8%
Burden	22%
Cost of Sales	75%
Gross Margin	25%
Selling	11%
G & A	9%
Total Selling G & A	20%
Pretax Profit	5%

A glance at Exhibit 4–1 should immediately make clear where your cost reduction efforts should be concentrated. Most company and division presidents, however, make two fundamental errors when first approaching cost reduction. They tend to place undue importance on attacking direct labor costs, and to feel that in order to remain competitive their companies must purchase new plants and equipment. For the average company, these are invariably two of the least effective areas to effect real savings. For virtually all companies, other options certainly should be pursued first.

There are no hidden tricks in determining where to concentrate your cost reduction efforts. The logic is simple: *Tackle first those areas where the largest sums of money are involved, for this is where the greatest savings can be effected.*

With this in mind, and using Exhibit 4–1 as a guide, determine the logical order of priorities for this typical metal fabricating company. At a glance it should be apparent that the priorities of this typical company should be set in the following order:

1. Material (45 percent)

2. Burden (22 percent)

3. Selling (11 percent)

4. G & A (9 percent)

5. Direct labor (8 percent)

Analysis of your own company's profit and loss statement may, of course, differ from the one outlined here. You may, for example, have other items to add to the list, such as research and development and debt service. But material costs will generally be your largest single percentage of sales, and direct labor one of the smallest (but don't forget the related fringes in the burden category). My management philosophy is that in most cases R & D should not be cut; in fact, I encourage managers to put some of their cost reduction savings into productive R & D projects.

Exhibit 4–2 clearly demonstrates the value of prioritizing your cost reduction efforts according to the direction of your cash outlay. Remember, the goal of any cost reduction program should be at least a 10 percent reduction in all costs. As illustrated in Exhibit 4–2, a 10 percent reduction in material costs would result in a savings of 4.5 percent of sales, while a 10 percent reduction in direct labor would result in only an .8 percent savings, or in selling costs only a 1.1 percent savings. In fact, in order to effect the same savings from a 10 percent reduction in material costs, direct labor would have to be reduced by almost 60 percent, a much more difficult, disruptive, and costly project unless your organization warrants it due to gross inefficiency. Note that with a 10 percent reduction in costs, profit increases much more than 10 percent. The gross margin in Exhibit 4-2 has increased 30 percent, and the pretax profit almost 300 percent!

Exhibit 4–2 The Priority of Cost Reduction

	Typical P & L, %	Priority of Attack	10% Cost Reduction Target, %	New P & L, %
Material	45	1	4.5	40.5
Direct Labor	8	5	.8	7.2
Burden	22	2	2.2	19.8
Cost of Sales	75			67.5
Gross Margin	25			32.5
Selling	11	3	1.1	9.9
G & A	9	4	.9	8.1
Pretax Profit	5			14.5

At this point you might wonder why material costs, which constitute the largest single cost factor in the typical manufacturing operation, were not included in your first month's "q and d" cost reduction program. The techniques required to reduce material costs are complicated, and must be maintained over a long period of time. They therefore have no place in a brief thirty-day introductory study except to analyze for pricing failures, as discussed in Chapter 10. Reducing material costs will, however, be discussed in detail in Chapters 6 and 7.

As mentioned, you will recognize the possible error of concentrating on cutting direct labor costs at the expense of, say, material and overhead (burden). Labor is the area where generally you will save the least, no matter how effective your program. There is undoubtedly slippage in your direct labor, but once a work sampling program is implemented it pays to relegate a more in-depth analysis of this area until the end of your full cost reduction program. There simply are far richer fields to harvest first. If, on the other hand, labor represents a large percentage of your company's total costs, it of course should become a higher cost reduction priority. In the majority of manufacturing companies, however, this is not the case.

The other fundamental mistake made by many managers in establishing cost reduction priorities is the desire to purchase new plants and equipment. While this indeed may reduce or eliminate some costs, it also will substantially increase burden through depreciation charges, and if done in large doses can negate much, if not all, apparent savings.

Purchasing new plants and equipment should be a last resort, when all other cost reduction options have been exhausted. Thus it is not until Chapter 11, entitled "Labor Costs and The New Industrial Revolution," that the parallel cost reduction techniques of reducing labor costs and automating your industrial operation are discussed.

Cost Reduction versus Growth

The often illusory benefits of purchasing new plants and equipment bring to mind perhaps the most dangerous fallacy of all: the emphasis on growth over cost reduction. It never should be forgotten that each added dollar in sales income costs a company money, both in outlay and commitment. Each dollar saved through cost reduction, on the other hand, costs very little. We have seen, for example, that a 10 percent across-the-board reduction in costs can almost triple your pretax profit. But how many dollars in increased sales would it take to increase your profit an equal amount?

Let's find out by using as an example a typical company doing $10,000,000 in sales, on which it realizes a pretax profit of 5 percent, and about 2.5 percent after tax net. Using the same figures we used earlier, costs are 95 percent of sales. A 10 percent reduction in costs would increase profits from $500,000 to $1,450,000 (or a $950,000 increase) because costs would be reduced from $9,500,000 to $8,550,000. This represents a 290 percent increase in pretax profit just from cost reduction.

In order to achieve the same 290 percent increase in pretax profit through an increase in sales, sales would have to be increased from their current $10,000,000 level to a whopping $29,000,000 (5 percent of $29,000,000 equals $1,450,000). This is a truly remarkable jump even in the best economic times and is not at all realistic for the vast majority of industrial companies. Actually, growth would have to be substantially more than 290 percent because debt would be created to handle the increase in working capital. This debt would create higher interest charges, which in turn would reduce profit. (This problem will be discussed in detail in the following section of this chapter.)

This does not mean to imply that there would be absolutely no savings during a period of growth. Savings would occur by better absorption of fixed burden, and possibly in general and administrative and selling costs. But the savings derived from such startling growth generally will not increase profit more than a percentage point, possibly two, and the strains on equipment and personnel will be monumental. With cost reduction, the savings and resulting profit improvement are immediate, dramatic, and relatively inexpensive. Furthermore, such savings do not require increased working capital or bank borrowings, or additional personnel, systems, plants, or equipment.

The Ultimate Liquidator: The Need for Working Capital in an Inflationary, High-Interest Economy

As difficult as a 290 percent increase in sales may be, even that may not accomplish our goal of increasing profits by $950,000. The previous discussion has not taken into account the need for more working capital to support sales growth, an immensely important factor, especially in these days of periodic high inflation and interest rates. Failure to recognize the need for increased working capital to support increased sales can quickly bring about the complete loss of profit. In fact, under our present corporate tax structure, as soon as inflation and interest rates rise simultaneously, bankruptcy becomes inevitable for thousands of small and medium size businesses, and for quite a few large companies as well.

Most of the adverse effects of high inflation and interest rates are well known and widely discussed. A tight money supply inhibits economic growth, which exacerbates unemployment; inflation erodes the purchasing power of the consumer's dollar, which in turn lowers our collective standard of living.

There is, however, a more insidious effect of the combination of high interest and inflation rates which ultimately is much more damaging to individual businesses, and thus to the U.S. economy as a whole. (This statement is applicable to other countries as well. While my studies have been applied only to the U.S. economy, they could be tailored to others.) The facts about these twin killers may be known, but it is remarkable that their most important ramifications are largely unrecognized and rarely discussed.

The problem is really quite simple. A typical manufacturing company often requires working capital of 40 to 45 percent of sales. Working capital is needed to pay for inventory and to support receivables, and usually includes a small amount of operating cash. As inflation increases the cost of doing business, the amount of working capital required also increases, even if the number of units sold remains constant or declines. In a period of high interest rates, the cost of borrowing in order to make available this additional capital eats into profits, and eventually will greatly deflate or eliminate profit and raise the debt-to-equity ratio to untenable levels.

Exhibit 4–3 demonstrates how in an 11 percent inflationary economy, with the prime interest rate at 16 percent, the profit as a percentage of sales of a $10 million company experiencing 12 percent annual unit growth will decrease from year to year. It is difficult to hit a moving target, so one tries for a middle ground in an example. An 11 percent inflation rate and a 16 percent prime may seem high by today's standards. It was not so long ago, however, that rates were much higher. Many observers, myself included, believe that if the U.S. government does not substantially reduce its budget deficit, we may soon again experience double-digit inflation along with significantly higher interest rates.

For the purpose of this discussion we also will assume that our prototypical company has working capital requirements of 40 percent of sales, an after-tax profit of 3.5 percent, a 25 percent annual dividend to shareholders, and an initial debt of $700,000. These numbers will vary, of course, for virtually every company in the United States, but they are fairly typical. We could have used as our example a much smaller company, or a much larger one. The dilemma would remain the same.

In calculating real interest rates, the banking practice of compensating balances usually must be taken into account. If, for example, a company borrows $1 million, the bank often will loan only $800,000, but will charge interest on $1 million, thereby increasing the real interest paid. If the company needs the full million, it pays interest on 120 percent of this amount. Thus, an 8 percent prime can actually become 9.6 percent, and in a far worse scenario, a 16 percent prime can jump to 19.2 percent.

Similarly, although inflation on all goods and services may be less than 10 percent, inflation on materials, which make up the bulk of most manufacturing companies' costs, can run at twice this rate. This is especially true for materials with a heavy basic metal content.

Exhibit 4–3 The Impact of 11 Percent Inflation and 19.2 Percent Effective Interest Rates

	Year 1	Year 2	Year 3	Year 4	Year 5	Year 6	Year 7
1. Units Sold	1,000,000	1,120,000	1,254,400	1,404,928	1,573,519	1,762,341	1,973,882
2. Selling Price of Units	$10.00	$11.10	$12.32	$13.68	$15.18	$16.85	$18.70
3. Total Sales	$10,000,000	$12,432,000	$15,455,462	$19,214,231	$23,887,126	$29,696,471	$36,918,654
4. Working Capital (at 40% of sales)	$4,000,000	$4,972,800	$6,182,185	$7,685,692	$9,554,850	$11,878,588	$14,767,462
5. Property, Plant, and Equipment			*Remains Equal to Depreciation Cash Flow*				
6. After-Tax Profit (at 3.5%)	$350,000	$435,120	$540,941	$672,498	$836,049	$1,039,376	$1,292,153
7. Shareholders' Dividend (at 25%)	$87,500	$108,780	$135,235	$168,125	$209,012	$259,844	$323,038
8. Available Profit (profit less shareholders' dividend)	$262,500	$326,340	$405,706	$504,373	$627,037	$779,532	$969,115
9. Yearly Increase in Working Capital		$972,800	$1,209,385	$1,503,507	$1,869,158	$2,323,738	$2,888,874
10. Yearly Shortfall		($710,300)	($1,018,434)	($1,330,959)	($1,725,716)	($2,223,300)	($2,849,378)

11. Cumulative Bank Borrowings to Make Up Previous Year's Shortfall	$700,000	$1,410,300	$2,428,734	$3,759,693	$5,485,409	$7,708,709	$10,558,087
12. Interest on Cumulative Shortfall at 19.2% (computed at 9.6% due to tax deduction)		$135,389	$233,158	$360,931	$526,599	$740,036	$1,013,576
13. Available for Reinvestment (profit less shareholders' dividend and interest costs)	$262,500	$190,951	$172,548	$143,442	$100,438	$39,496	($44,461)
14. Equity (end of year)	$2,000,000	$2,262,500	$2,453,451	$2,625,999	$2,769,441	$2,869,879	$2,909,375
15. Incremental Debt-to-Equity Ratio		2.71 to 1	5.33 to 1	7.71 to 1	12.03 to 1	22.14 to 1	72.14 to 1
16. Cumulative Debt-to-Equity Ratio	0.35 to 1	0.62 to 1	0.99 to 1	1.43 to 1	1.98 to 1	2.69 to 1	3.63 to 1
17. Real After-Tax Profit (after-tax profit less after-tax interest costs)	$350,000	$299,731	$307,783	$311,567	$309,450	$299,340	$278,577
18. After-Tax Profit as a Percentage of Sales	3.50%	2.41%	1.99%	1.62%	1.30%	1.01%	0.75%

Inflation	11%	After-Tax Profit as a % of Sales	3.5%
Prime	16%	Share Dividend as a % of After-Tax Profits	25%
Pretax Interest Rate	19.2%	Starting Equity	$2,000,000
After-Tax Interest Rate	9.6%	Starting Unit Volume	1,000,000
Real Annual Unit Growth	12%	Starting Unit Price	$10.00
Working Capital as a % of Sales	40%	Starting Debt	$700,000

For our purposes, therefore, we have assumed 19.2 percent interest (including compensating balance costs) and 11 percent inflation. Your own numbers may vary, of course, but this illustration will permit you to recognize the problem and its potential ramifications. And again, remember that while interest rates may be substantially lower than this today, given the current economic situation one cannot assume they will remain low. And besides, even during moderate inflationary conditions, the cost of certain key items can skyrocket. For example, during one recent period of less than 5 percent inflation, a certain medium-size manufacturer of baseball gloves saw the price of leather suddenly jump 30 percent.

In Year 1, this typical $10 million manufacturing company requires $4,000,000 for working capital and has an after-tax profit of $350,000 (3.5 percent). Normally, one can expect a company to dividend 30 to 35 percent of after-tax profit to its shareholders, but in our example we have only allocated $87,500 (25 percent) in order to conserve as much of our earnings for working capital as possible. $262,500 ($350,000 less $87,500) will then be available for reinvestment. This example also assumes that depreciation cash flow is sufficient to pay for capital needs, a dangerous assumption if inflation takes off.

In Year 2, costs have increased 11 percent for our prototypal $10 million company, so prices must also increase 11 percent. To do otherwise would be suicidal. In addition, the company has experienced 12 percent growth, so it now sells 1,120,000 units instead of the 1,000,000 it sold in Year 1. Total sales are therefore $12,432,000 in Year 2, and the company needs an additional $972,800 (40 percent of the sales increase) in working capital. $262,500 is available for reinvestment from Year 1 profits, leaving a shortfall of $710,300 ($972,800 less $262,500).

This $710,300 cannot come from depreciation of equipment, at least not for long, because machinery continually has to be replaced, and it generally costs at least three times what it did when originally purchased. In periods of high inflation and/or recession, raising money in the bond market or with preferred or common stock is generally out of the question for the average company. Many companies resort to selling off real estate or their lower-yield divisions in order to come up with necessary working capital, but there is obviously a limit to these resources. A company in need of cash also can attempt to manage its existing working capital better, but again this only postpones the problem a few years at most. Still other companies will be forced to reduce or eliminate dividends to shareholders or to cut back on badly needed capital expenditures. Not only are these solutions shortsighted, they also in the end cost the United States economy jobs and delay desperately needed modernization.

In many cases, therefore, the only recourse will be the banks, where a $710,300 loan at 19.2 percent will cost $136,378 in interest payments alone, with little hope of paying off the principal. In Year 2, about half of this interest payment (9.6 percent) will have to be deducted from the company's after-tax profit. This $68,189 in interest payments must be added to the existing payments of $67,200 (.096 x the existing debt of $700,000) for a total payment of $135,389 ($68,189 + $67,200). This leaves only $190,951 for reinvestment in Year 3 ($326,340–$135,389).

As demonstrated by Exhibit 4–3, the company's situation worsens each year. By Year 4, the company has grown to almost $20 million in sales, with working capital requirements of more than $7.6 million. Debt has grown from $700,000 in Year 1 to a whopping $3.75 million, with a cumulative debt-to-equity ratio of 1.43 to 1. Even more disturbing is the fact that the company's incremental debt-to-equity ratio during the second year is already well over one to one. The company is immediately borrowing more money than it is retaining from its earnings. A healthy company should try to earn at least three or four dollars for every dollar it borrows. In Year 5, our prototypic company is borrowing $12.03 for every dollar it supplies.

In other words, line 15 in Exhibit 4–3 is a warning that the company is in immediate trouble in Year 2, as soon as it begins to borrow money in order to meet its expanding working capital requirements; line 16 shows that at the end of the third year, when cumulative debt to equity is approaching one to one, the company has possibly passed the point of no return.

In the final analysis, the seriousness of this company's situation is dramatically demonstrated by the fact that after-tax profit as a percentage of sales has decreased from a respectable 3.5 percent in Year 1 to a subpar 1.62 percent in Year 4. In fact, in Year 7 this company has virtually no profit available for reinvestment and has a debt-to-equity ratio of four to one, which of course would be unacceptable to the banks or bond rating agencies.

Within four years the company has grown about 200 percent in sales dollars—from $10 million to almost $20 million—but has actually reduced its profit by almost $40,000. In only a few short years, this company is heavily in debt, has a poor profit position, and will have to sell, close, or retract its operations in an effort to restore itself to a healthy position.

Particularly in recent years, inflation and interest rates have been volatile, and cannot be predicted with any certainty. Exhibits 4–4, 4–5, and 4–6, however, graphically illustrate that companies can experience difficulties even if both interest and inflation rates are much lower.

Exhibit 4–4, for example, shows that even with a prime rate of 10 percent and a cost escalation (inflation) factor of only 9 percent, real profit as a percentage of sales decreases from year to year. Using the worst case shown, (a 20 percent prime and 15 percent cost escalation), a company's profit would be entirely dissipated in less than five years.

Exhibit 4–4 Real Profit as a Percentage of Sales with 12 Percent Unit Growth

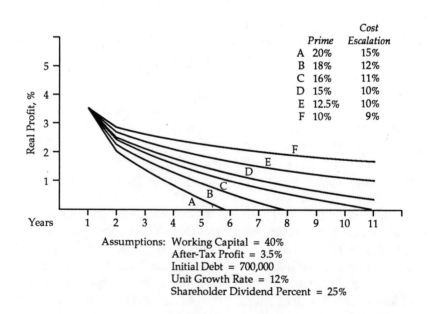

Assumptions: Working Capital = 40%
After-Tax Profit = 3.5%
Initial Debt = 700,000
Unit Growth Rate = 12%
Shareholder Dividend Percent = 25%

Exhibit 4–5 Total (Cumulative) Debt-to-Equity Ratios with 12 Percent Unit Growth

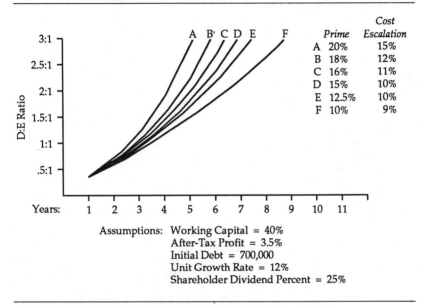

	Prime	Cost Escalation
A	20%	15%
B	18%	12%
C	16%	11%
D	15%	10%
E	12.5%	10%
F	10%	9%

Assumptions: Working Capital = 40%
After-Tax Profit = 3.5%
Initial Debt = 700,000
Unit Growth Rate = 12%
Shareholder Dividend Percent = 25%

In part, the dire situation illustrated in Exhibits 4–4 and 4–5 was due to the 12 percent unit growth built into the analysis. In fact, however, a company can find itself in trouble even without growth and even if it begins with absolutely no debt. Few companies today have the luxury of no debt.

Exhibits 4–7, 4–8, 4–9, and 4–10 demonstrate this problem clearly. They show, for example, that with a prime and a cost escalation factor of 17.5 percent, a company starting with no debt and no unit growth will quickly be in trouble, particularly if it is not able to reduce working capital requirements, even with no initial debt and no unit growth. Note that Exhibits 4–7 and 4–8 demonstrate that in only five years a company's cumulative debt-to-equity ratio will equal and then far exceed our one-to-one maximum target.

Although Exhibits 4–7 through 4–10 demonstrate that limiting a company's growth by no means automatically negates the twin problems of high inflation and high interest rates, a no-growth policy will help prevent the problem from getting completely out of hand as it was in the real growth example depicted in Exhibit 4–1.

Exhibit 4–6 Incremental Debt-to-Equity Ratios with 12 Percent Unit Growth

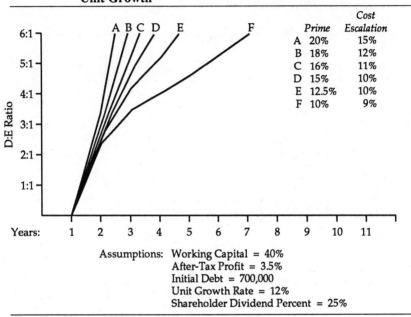

Assumptions: Working Capital = 40%
After-Tax Profit = 3.5%
Initial Debt = 700,000
Unit Growth Rate = 12%
Shareholder Dividend Percent = 25%

Exhibit 4–7 Real Profit as a Percentage of Sales with No Unit Growth

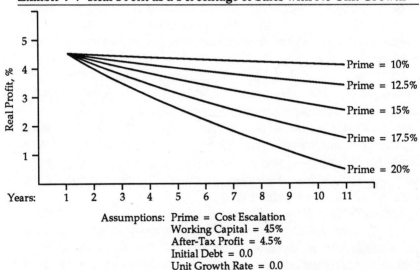

Assumptions: Prime = Cost Escalation
Working Capital = 45%
After-Tax Profit = 4.5%
Initial Debt = 0.0
Unit Growth Rate = 0.0
Shareholder Dividend Percent = 20%

Exhibit 4–8 Total Cumulative Debt-to-Equity Ratios with No Unit Growth

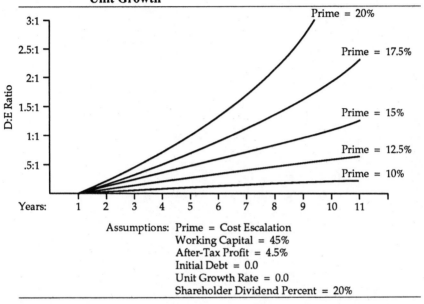

Assumptions: Prime = Cost Escalation
Working Capital = 45%
After-Tax Profit = 4.5%
Initial Debt = 0.0
Unit Growth Rate = 0.0
Shareholder Dividend Percent = 20%

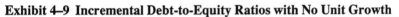

Exhibit 4–9 Incremental Debt-to-Equity Ratios with No Unit Growth

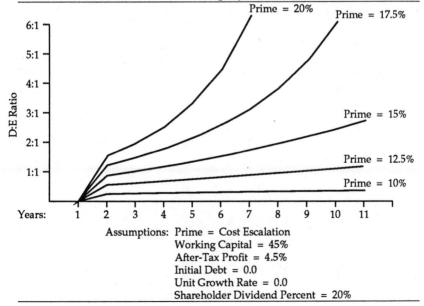

Assumptions: Prime = Cost Escalation
Working Capital = 45%
After-Tax Profit = 4.5%
Initial Debt = 0.0
Unit Growth Rate = 0.0
Shareholder Dividend Percent = 20%

Exhibit 4–10 The Impact of 17.5 Percent Inflation and 21 Percent Effective Interest Rates

	Year 1	Year 2	Year 3	Year 4	Year 5	Year 6	Year 7
1. Units Sold	1,000,000	1,000,000	1,000,000	1,000,000	1,000,000	1,000,000	1,000,000
2. Selling Price of Units	10.00	11.75	13.81	16.22	19.06	22.40	26.32
3. Total Sales	10,000,000	11,750,000	13,806,250	16,222,344	19,061,254	22,396,973	26,316,444
4. Working Capital (at 45% of sales)	4,500,000	5,287,500	6,212,813	7,300,055	8,577,564	10,078,638	11,842,400
5. Property, Plant, and Equipment			*Remains Equal to Depreciation Cash Flow*				
6. After-Tax Profit (at 4.5%)	450,000	528,750	621,281	730,005	857,756	1,007,864	1,184,240
7. Shareholders' Dividend (at 20%)	90,000	105,750	124,256	146,001	171,551	201,573	236,848
8. Available Profit (profit less shareholders' dividend)	300,000	423,000	497,025	584,004	686,205	806,291	947,392
9. Yearly Increase in Working Capital		787,500	925,313	1,087,242	1,277,509	1,501,074	1,763,762
10. Yearly Shortfall		(427,500)	(547,201)	(692,561)	(868,568)	(1,081,131)	(1,337,252)

11. Cumulative Bank Borrowings to Make Up Previous Year's Shortfall	0	427,500	974,701	1,667,262	2,535,830	3,616,961	4,954,213
12. Interest on Cumulative Shortfall at 21% (computed at 10.5% due to tax deduction)		44,888	102,344	175,063	266,262	379,781	520,192
13. Available for Reinvestment (profit less shareholders' dividend and interest costs)	360,000	378,112	394,681	408,941	419,943	426,510	427,200
14. Equity (end of year)	2,000,000	2,360,000	2,738,112	3,132,793	3,541,734	3,961,677	4,388,187
15. Incremental Debt-to-Equity Ratio		1.19	1.45	1.75	2.12	2.57	3.14
16. Cumulative Debt-to-Equity Ratio	0.00	0.18	0.36	0.53	0.72	0.91	1.13
17. Real After-Tax Profit (after-tax profit less after-tax interest costs)	450,000	483,862	518,937	554,942	591,494	628,083	664,048
18. After-Tax Profit as a Percentage of Sales	4.50	4.12	3.76	3.42	3.10	2.80	2.52

Inflation	17.5%	Real Annual Unit Growth	0
Prime	17.5%	Working Capital as a % of Sales	45%
Pretax Interest Rate	21%	After-Tax Profit as a % of Sales	4.5%
After-Tax Interest Rate	10.5%	Share Dividend as a % of After-Tax Profits	20%

Starting Equity	$2,000,000
Starting Unit Volume	1,000,000
Starting Unit Price	$10
Starting Debt	0

It is difficult, however, to tell American executives that at all costs their businesses must not increase sales. Free enterprise economic philosophy has always preached that growth is the most desirable goal possible. Can it really be that in an inflationary economy a company must remain stagnant or regress to have any hope of surviving?

Sadly, during periods of high inflation and high prime rates, the answer for working capital intensive companies, at least temporarily, is yes. The combined effect of high inflation and interest rates tends to insidiously eat away at profits, and in many cases makes growth suicidal. It is no wonder that during periods of high inflation we see so many bankruptcies, mergers, and companies up for sale. In 1982, for example, bankruptcies occurred at the highest rate since records were initiated in 1941. Even some of our giant corporations such as General Motors, Chrysler and International Harvester (Navistar) were forced to sell profitable divisions or dispose of assets in order to come up with desperately needed working capital. The same thing will certainly happen if and when, as many economists fear, we again experience double-digit inflation and interest rates.

The first step toward a solution to this dilemma is simply to recognize that it exists, so that whenever inflation rates begin to rise the problem can be attacked head-on. An economy cannot continue to function indefinitely under the twin stresses of double-digit inflation and interest rates. Nor can it use capital for long overdue modernization when every available dollar is needed for working capital.

Put another way, in an inflationary economy it takes almost 10 percent net after-tax income (more than twice the current national average) and no increase in the dividend percent ratio to stay even in a no unit growth sales market (yet the national average is approximately 4.5 percent).

Summary

In summary, there are a variety of specific actions which can be taken that will avoid, or at least delay, the scenarios detailed here. During periods of high inflation and high interest rates, chief executives should:

1. Streamline their entire organization through a comprehensive cost reduction program. Build profits through cost reduction, as opposed to unit growth.

2. Evaluate their respective companies to determine their own particular figures and how their need for working capital is affecting them in an inflationary and high-interest economy.

3. Consider maintaining no growth, or at least limiting growth, until the inflationary climate and/or their own profit levels improve.

4. Sell off or close down marginally profitable or red ink operations in order to free up working capital.

5. To the extent possible, eliminate short-term debt and replace it with some kind of a fixed long-term debt. This would be particularly appropriate during breaks in the interest rates.

6. Reduce working capital whenever and wherever possible by becoming much more strict on accounts receivable and/or improving management of inventory.

7. Most importantly, continually remind legislators concerning the need for a 30 to 35 percent tax rate for industry so that working capital can be replenished. Higher earnings resulting from a lower tax rate would tend to increase the equity market and permit equity financing to pay off short-term debt.

In the early 1930s, industry had little short-term debt and was coming off a decade of strong earnings and a strong stock market. Therefore, when the depression hit, receivables were collected and cash was available to sustain companies during the bad period. Today, however, industry is heavily in short-term debt. If a depression hit now, the cash from receivables would have to be used to pay off short-term bank debt. Industry would be much more vulnerable; many businesses would fail; pension plans, where they already are poorly financed, would be a disaster area; the Pension Benefit Guaranty Corporation would be bankrupt; and the country would be in financial chaos.

In short, unless the difficulty of maintaining profitability and at the same time obtaining working capital under the double stress of high inflation and high interest rates is finally recognized and remedial action taken, I am afraid that during the next period of high rates the flurry of bankruptcies we witnessed during the late seventies and early eighties will seem mild in comparison.

5

Ranking of Activities

N ow that you are aware of the priorities of cost reduction, it is important to make certain that you and your division or department heads are spending the greatest amount of time and energy in those areas that can effect the greatest reductions in cost. Remember, your priorities relate to your own expense categories. The ordered priorities in our example remain:

1. Materials

2. Burden

3. Selling

4. General and administrative

5. Direct labor

Ranking Departmental Areas

A large diversified corporation recently convened its division heads for an in-depth discussion of mutual goals and problems. The chief executive officer distributed a questionnaire designed to determine in which areas these top managers—all highly qualified people—had been concentrating their efforts during the past year. They were requested to rate their own priorities.

Exhibit 5–1 is a specimen of a questionnaire from which division presidents or managers can make records of how they spend their time. In one respect it is a self-evaluating time and motion study. As you can

Exhibit 5–1 Ranking of Activities

Name _____   Division _____

Indicate the percentage of your time spent in each of the following individual categories, and rank the subcategories. Then describe the reasons for the emphasis indicated within each category:

Personnel: _____%   Performance appraisal   _____
                                   Selection   _____
                                   Training   _____
                                   Development   _____
                                   Other (specify activity) _____
Describe emphasis: _____

Marketing and sales: _____%   Long-range strategy   _____
                                   Short-term planning   _____
                                   Short-term accomplishments   _____
                                   Selling   _____
                                   Customer relations/services   _____
                                   Advertising   _____
                                   Promotion   _____
                                   Other (specify activity)   _____
Describe emphasis: _____

Cost reduction: _____%   Ratio analysis   _____
                                   Methods improvement   _____
                                   Value analysis   _____
                                   Redesign for cost reduction _____
                                   Work sampling   _____
                                   Time and motion study   _____
                                   Other (specify activity)   _____
Describe emphasis: _____

Exhibit 5–1 (continued)

Asset control:	_____%	Cash management	_____
		Inventory	_____
		Receivables	_____
		Capital expenditures	_____
		Other (specify activity)	_____
Describe emphasis:		_____	

Manufacturing:	_____%	Supervisory meetings	_____
		Time spent in work areas	_____
		Union activities	_____
		Quality review	_____
		Engineering-manufacturing, obsolescence committee	_____
		Process improvement	_____
		Other (specify activity)	_____
Describe emphasis:		_____	

Long-range planning:	_____%	Facilities planning	_____
		New markets	_____
		Internal growth	_____
		New product development	_____
		Existing product modification	_____
		Personnel development	_____
		Other (specify activity)	_____
Describe emphasis:		_____	

Purchasing:	_____%	Effectiveness review	_____
		Vendor relations	_____
		Problem areas	_____
		Make or buy analysis	_____
		Vendor sourcing	_____
		Other (specify activity)	_____
Describe emphasis:		_____	

Other significant tasks:	_____%	_____	_____
		_____	_____
		_____	_____
		_____	_____
Describe emphasis:		_____	

Total of activities must equal 100 percent.

see, the coverage ranges from the percentage of time spent on personnel, to the percentage required for marketing and sales, cost reduction, asset control, manufacturing, long-range planning, purchasing, and other significant tasks. The latter miscellaneous category recognizes the fact that there are unplanned and unscheduled calls upon the time of any chief operating officer. The questionnaire surveys the percentage of time executives spend on each problem and consideration. It also breaks down the time spent on each category.

In pencil, complete the questionnaire in Exhibit 5–1. (If you are not now a manager, rank your activities as you would plan them if you were managing a company.) Then study Exhibit 5–2 to see how the division presidents of the diversified company we spoke of earlier rated their own time, both the first year they were asked to fill out the questionnaire, and in the second year. These results are expressed in percentages of their respective times.

Based on the priorities emphasized in this guide, from Exhibit 5–2 can you identify areas of misspent time recorded for the first year and areas of improvement in the second year? Are you able to spot existing dangers?

In listing divisions *under* their previous year's budget and divisions *over* their previous year's budget, we refer, respectively, to those that are operating *under* budget, with lower than projected profit, and those operating *over* budget, showing a better than projected profit.

Before continuing, study Exhibit 5–2 and try to determine where these managers are failing to establish proper priorities.

What shows up most clearly in the recapitulation is that the heads of the divisions with less that $10,000,000 in sales were spending 32 percent of their time on marketing and sales, while those with more than $10,000,000 in sales were spending only 20 percent of their time on marketing. Heads of divisions that were failing to make their profit targets were spending 29 percent of their time on the selling effort, while those over budget on profits were devoting 23 percent to marketing and sales. It is clear from this data that the heads of these smaller companies and those behind budget were "out on the road," so to speak, and were not spending a sufficient amount of their time and energies being efficient executives. They perceived sales and marketing as their primary area of concentration, which, while a fact of life, can tend to minimize or exclude other key areas that need their active participation and direction.

Exhibit 5–2 Activity Ranking of Division Presidents

	Personnel	Marketing & Sales	Cost Reduction	Asset Control	Manu-facturing	Long-Range Planning	Pur-chasing	Other
Year 1								
All Divisions	10	26	10	10	16	12	8	3
Divisions over $10 million	12	20	10	10	16	13	9	10
Divisions under $10 million	9	32	9	9	16	12	7	6
Divisions over Previous Year's Budget	11	23	10	10	13	11	9	13
Divisions under Previous Year's Budget	10	29	10	9	18	13	7	4
Year 2								
All Divisions	10	23	13	12	15	13	10	4
Divisions over $10 million	11	18	15	12	13	16	10	5
Divisions under $10 million	9	29	11	11	16	11	10	3
Divisions over Previous Year's Budget	11	24	13	11	13	15	9	4
Divisions under Previous Year's Budget	8	23	12	13	16	12	12	4

By the end of the second year, the presidents of the divisions doing less than $10,000,000 were spending less of their time, 29 percent, on marketing and sales. At the same time, they increased from 9 percent to 11 percent the amount of time they spent on cost reduction. Perhaps they had begun to be aware of that fundamental truth of business management: *Cost reduction is a surer way to improve profits than an increase in sales. But the time they spent on cost reduction was still far too low.*

Significantly, the presidents of divisions with more than $10,000,000 in sales who had spent 10 percent of their time on cost reduction in the first year increased their concentration on cost reduction by five points in the second year to 15 percent of their available time.

In both the companies with less than $10,000,000 in sales and those with more, the managers, in their second year of rating themselves, were being better executives. It is noteworthy, however, that the executives in the larger companies continued to budget their time better than those in the smaller ones. They also placed greater emphasis on cost reduction.

Another indication that the presidents of both the larger and smaller companies were gaining a better perspective on their roles is that they spent more time on asset control and purchasing in the second year than they did in the first. But again, they didn't spend nearly as much time as they should.

One conclusion that can be made from these tabulations is that the chief executives of smaller companies, with sales under $10,000,000, are worried about sales and feel compelled to give it maximum effort. As a result, they are not minding the store, while their more successful counterparts are taking the time to be more efficient executives. Executives of smaller companies are trying to improve sales rather than profits. They are not concentrating on the areas of cost reduction and purchasing that would give them a better chance to improve profits. In the first year, the presidents of the larger divisions were spending 9 percent of their time on purchasing, and those heading the smaller companies were giving the subject only 7 percent of their time.

Purchasing has been emphasized because this is the department in charge of buying parts and materials, and, as we learned previously, in most manufacturing companies material constitutes the single largest

cost—from 40 to 50 percent—of sales. Furthermore, inventory generally represents a company's largest asset investment.

As purchasing is a real hunting ground for corporate profit improvement, and an area that is shortchanged by many manufacturing companies, Chapters 6 and 7 are devoted to an in-depth discussion of
specific purchasing and material categorizing techniques that can substantially cut costs.

Before going on to that, however, let us further investigate how time
should be spent in the cost reduction area, using the same company as
we did in Exhibits 5–1 and 5–2 as an example. Since Exhibit 5–2
revealed that none of the division heads was spending sufficient time
on cost reduction, it is enlightening to see how these managers ranked
themselves in giving consideration to the various elements of a cost
reduction program.

Six Cost Reduction Techniques

Exhibit 5–3 lists six basic techniques for cost reduction, and requires
executives to show how much time they spent on ratio analysis,
methods improvement, value analysis, redesign for cost reduction,
work sampling, and time and motion studies. Organization analysis was
omitted from this particular exercise.

Exhibit 5–3 presents the average ranking given to six basic cost
reduction techniques by the division presidents. The order is listed so
that number 1 is ranked as the first order of importance and number 6
as the least order of importance—the category receiving the least
amount of their time and attention.

This is the rank of importance they gave to cost reduction techniques:

1. Methods improvement

2. Value analysis

3. Redesign

4. Work sampling

5. Ratio analysis

6. Time and motion study

Exhibit 5-3 Ranking of Cost Reduction Activities

	Ratio Analysis	Methods Improvements	Value Analysis	Redesign for Cost Reduction	Work Sampling	Time & Motion Study
Year 1						
All Divisions	5	1	2	3	4	6
Divisions over $10 million	5	2	1	3	4	6
Divisions under $10 million	4	1	2	3	6	5
Divisions over Budget	6	2	1	3	4	5
Divisions under Budget	4	1	3	2	6	5
Year 2						
All Divisions	1	2	4	3	5	6
Divisions over $10 million	1	2	4	3	5	6
Divisions under $10 million	2	1	4	3	5	6
Divisions over Budget	1	2	4	3	5	6
Divisions under Budget	2	1	3	4	5	6

The heads of divisions earning less than $10,000,000 in sales gave this ranking:

1. Methods improvement
2. Value analysis
3. Redesign
4. Ratio analysis
5. Time and motion study
6. Work sampling

Almost all of the executives were doing the wrong things! Methods improvement is the least rewarding, least effective area in which to devote time for quick cost reduction, yet it had top priority among division presidents, each of whom headed an operation sorely in need of cost reduction programs. Moreover, the comments they made on their questionnaires showed that they were seeking to solve their problems through machine methods, which experience clearly shows is one of the slowest and most costly methods, as will be discussed in later chapters.

You will note that heads of divisions operating below expected profit had no comprehension of how to approach cost reduction. They listed work sampling, for example, as the least important technique. Ratio analysis, which should have been ranked number 1, was ranked fourth; value analysis, which like methods improvement is effective only over a long period of time, was ranked third; redesign, which takes even more time than value analysis to show results, was ranked second; work sampling, which is part of our immediately beneficial "quick and dirty" program, was ranked last; and time and motion study, which takes up to eighteen months to complete and should have been in the sixth position, was ranked fifth.

Upon further investigation of all the completed questionnaires, it quickly became clear that not one of the presidents knew how to spend time to most effectively cut costs. These are top-flight managers, representative of U.S. industry, and they provide us with proof that a high percentage of those who are running U.S. companies do not know how to pursue cost reduction quickly and effectively.

Not one of these presidents was giving priority to the "quick and dirty" cost reduction techniques, as outlined in the first three chapters of this text. Yet this is the place where cost reduction must start. It is no wonder that so many companies fail during recessions.

In all fairness, they did begin to understand the importance of ratio analysis between year 1 and 2. But work sampling, redesign, and value analysis were never really properly recognized as important cost reduction tools in either year.

Rate yourself objectively in all these categories. This is yet another technique that should be repeated year after year.

III

Areas of
Concentration

6

Emphasis on Purchasing

In previous chapters we have demonstrated that immediate and substantial savings can be made through an intensive, thirty-day cost
reduction effort, and that the first step toward longer-range cost reduction is to prioritize target areas.

The value of cost reduction, rather than growth, has also been emphasized. In Chapter 4 we mentioned that growth is expensive, that in
order to increase sales a company may be burdened with a variety of
additional expenses. More employees may have to be hired, prices may
have to be reduced or held flat, facilities expanded, and substantial increases will have to be made in working capital, resulting in high interest costs which eat into profit. Recall that in Chapter 4, in the section
entitled "Cost Reduction versus Growth," it was demonstrated that even
in the best circumstances, a $10 million company would have to in-
crease sales to $29 million, or by 290 percent, in order to effect the same
increase in profit that could be gained through a simple 10 percent cost
reduction program; and even this is questionable when one realizes that
the interest costs necessary to support such growth would cut into
profits.

Growth, in other words, is expensive. Cost reduction, on the other
hand, costs virtually nothing, except sometimes your personal
popularity and "good guy" image. But, as the supervising partner on my

first consulting assignment told me years ago, "We're paid to get results, not win popularity contests." The same is true in management.

Previous chapters have also emphasized that since the purchasing department can control 40 to 50 percent of your sales dollar (see Exhibit 6–1), cutting material costs can have the greatest benefit to a company's performance. Furthermore, the cost of materials can be reduced with existing personnel, and frequently without additional expense or investment. This is perhaps the single most important message to be found anywhere in this text: Material is almost always the area where the greatest savings can be realized, and the savings can be obtained by focusing on purchasing, aided by engineering and manufacturing.

Exhibit 6–1 Typical Cost Breakdown

Type of Industry: Manufacturing (light)

Sales	$20 million
Material	45%
Direct Labor	8%
Burden	22%
Cost of Sales	75%
General and Administrative	9%
Selling	11%
Total Selling G & A	20%
Total Costs	95%
Pretax Profit	5%

The reason I am such a strong believer that purchasing is the area where the greatest cost cutting successes can be realized is not because I worked my way up through this area. On the contrary. My own early background was in sales and manufacturing. I did, however, witness the development of purchasing into a science in the early Thirties by observing the automotive companies to which my father sold. Ultimately, however, it is the profit and loss statement that convinced me of the importance of purchasing in any effort to reduce costs.

Key Purchasing Principles

Although the simple principle of purchasing a specified material at the least expensive price from qualified vendors might seem like an obvious goal, the importance of meeting this goal is almost never truly recognized by top management. Management frequently gives lip service to this definition of the purchasing function, but they do not really understand that proper purchasing techniques can turn red ink to black. Most top executives also fail to recognize that there is no better way to affect profitability positively. These attitudes are usually due to management's general unfamiliarity with purchasing.

This chapter begins by emphasizing the importance of treating the purchasing department as an instrumental part of any cost reduction effort. There are three overall key purchasing principles that must be recognized and understood by all top executives:

1. *Don't Be Afraid of the Purchasing Department*

   Many company or division presidents are not acquainted with the purchasing function. Take the time to learn the various cost reduction opportunities discussed in this chapter. Make certain that your top management spends time learning about purchasing. And above all, don't isolate yourself from your purchasing department and your head of purchasing. Become involved.

2. *Concentrate Efforts on "A" Parts*

   In most instances, 5 to 10 percent of all manufacturing parts and materials make up approximately 70 to 75 percent of total material costs. Make certain your purchasing department spends the great majority of its time on the selection, delivery and turnover of these more expensive "A" parts. Effective procurement, substitution, or redesign will have the greatest impact in this area.

   By providing an overall picture of material costs, indexing "A" parts will also serve as a guideline for pricing decisions.

3. *Purchase; Don't Expedite*

   Your purchasing department should be allowed to use its creativity, imagination, and professional experience to purchase parts and material at the lowest possible prices. Don't treat your purchasing department as if you were ordering out for coffee. Don't put them into an expediting mode by poor forecasting (see Chapter 9) or lack of proper sales and manufacturing planning.

After discussing these general, overall principles, the chapter then details six specific purchasing techniques:

1. Utilizing an ABC stratification system (established by your inventory planning and control department)
2. Encouraging competition among vendors
3. Avoiding single-sourced items
4. Standardizing materials
5. Negotiating with suppliers
6. Insisting on high integrity of the purchasing staff

The chapter concludes with a detailed discussion of longer term purchasing goals.

Direct Access for a Managerial Function

In all too many instances, the company president is reluctant to get involved with purchasing due to a lack of understanding of that particular department. This lack of understanding stems from the fact that company presidents rarely seem to have a purchasing background. They are much more likely to have worked in sales, manufacturing, engineering, or accounting. Executives tend to supervise most closely the area (or areas) with which they are most familiar, often at the expense of purchasing. This is a serious mistake. In order to combat this tendency, purchasing should be a required part of any executive training program. By the same token, purchasing personnel should receive training and practical experience in accounting, manufacturing, and engineering in order to broaden their knowledge and awareness.

The first step toward creating an effective purchasing policy is to make certain that there is direct access between the company or division president and the head of purchasing. The purchasing chief should have the ear and confidence of top management. This individual should be considered a top department head. After all, the purchasing supervisor frequently controls the largest share of the company's money.

The purchasing department can and should provide direct, important input to the company president from the front lines when it comes to such decisions as make-or-buy, redesign, vendor selection, alternate sourcing, availability, and pricing. This department can also be of great help in keeping investment down, inventories balanced, and run-outs minimized. Too frequently, however, the purchasing department is relegated to an expediting function due to poor planning and/or poor inventory records and controls.

By having the purchasing department report directly to the division or company president, any change in material costs, deliveries, market trends, or possible component substitution can be evaluated quickly so that the best possible business decisions can be made. A weekly or monthly report should be generated by the purchasing department and sent to the company or division head. This report should summarize weekly or monthly activities and emphasize recent price increases and cost reduction (as well as cost avoidance) successes. If a 10 percent reduction in material costs has been established as the company's objective, this report should analyze how well this goal is being met. Especially in periods of inflation, a weekly cost index of key (or "A") parts is essential in developing intelligent and timely pricing moves to help protect profit margins.

This book's recommendation that the purchasing director report directly to the company head runs contrary to a concept that has been gaining in popularity—the institution of a materials manager. While there are exceptions, in the vast majority of cases this type of position is not a good idea in small and medium-size companies. First of all, it downgrades purchasing to one or two levels below the company head so that the steward of your main cost segment is now reporting to a materials manager, who frequently reports to the head of manufacturing. Demoting the purchasing department two levels puts a lower salary level on the job and makes it subject to pressures from people who are frequently interested in output regardless of outcome. As a result, the purchasing job is degraded to expediting.

Secondly, creating a one-over-two supervisory position (instead of our sought-after one-over-seven to ten suggested in Chapter 1) defies good organizational practice. In addition, a materials manager who has come up through production control generally won't have the necessary background to supervise purchasing intelligently. I've never seen manufacturing and sales under one department head. In my judgment, procurement is equally foreign to production control, especially as a company grows and becomes more complex. Do not sacrifice your materials area by failing to make certain that your materials manager is competent in the procurement field.

Purchase; Don't Expedite

A company president should be certain of the caliber and integrity of the purchasing staff, and should make them feel a part of the management team working to keep costs down. All too often, purchasing is treated as a perfunctory, clerical, or expediting function.

In analyzing a purchasing department's effectiveness, you must answer one simple question: Is it a clerical operation or a professional one? Does the purchasing manager have the necessary authority to make management decisions? Anyone, if told to do so, can send out a purchase order to a given vendor for a specific part. But a purchasing manager should be able to do much more than that by taking into account the many variables that enter into most any purchasing agreement. The purchasing manager should, for example, be able to suggest to management that a savings could be made by purchasing from one of the company's other divisions; or by changing vendors; or in another case by manufacturing the part in-house; or that by buying in volume now, the immediate cost savings will offset the cost of carrying it in inventory. Or perhaps the total purchase can be made but delivery taken in monthly quantities.

If people are treated like clerks, they will become clerks. If they are treated like professionals, they have the opportunity to become professionals. When the purchasing staff knows they are valued for the special skills they possess and are encouraged to think like managers, they become an immensely valuable asset to the company.

Along these same lines, a purchasing department must be given the freedom and time span to use its cost cutting skills. If the sales or manufacturing department demands a volume of parts for immediate delivery, the hands of the purchasing chief are tied. Not only will the purchasing department be unable to negotiate the best price, but every aspect of making that part available will be unnecessarily costly. Transportation and packaging costs will be at a premium, and there certainly won't be time to sit down with the sales, manufacturing, and engineering departments to make any kind of redesign or needs-versus-costs analysis. In addition, economic order quantities, proper sourcing, negotiated contracts, and suggested improvements won't be possible.

A purchasing staff should not, in other words, simply be told to order a given number of parts. Rather, they should be told that a specific number of these parts are needed over a particular period of time, and asked to come up with recommendations on how best to obtain them. Now the buyers can negotiate with outside vendors not as if they were routinely ordering out for coffee, but rather by conducting a proper sourcing job based on the item's required quality, volume, and delivery; previous prices; possible lower-priced substitutes; and the best manufacturing and vending methods.

In order to emphasize the importance of the purchasing department being comprised of skilled individuals, buyers can and should be rotated from assignment to assignment. Wherever possible, buyers should also be rotated between such disciplines as industrial engineering, inventory and production control, and accounting. These rotating practices will ensure that buyers do not become stale and that they have the broad experience necessary to understand the various cost reduction techniques and the impact of their decisions. Most important, they will feel they are a valuable and integral part of the company. Rotation will also eliminate the likelihood of an individual buying from certain vendors over a long period of time and thereby establishing a personal, rather than a business, relationship with that vendor.

(Rotation of responsibilities should not be limited to the purchasing area. It should be instituted among all capable newcomers in a company. It will allow them a better overall knowledge of the organization, which is so useful once they reach the executive level, and will enable them to identify the areas they enjoy the most and in which they are most capable).

Since the purchasing staff are trained to interface with the outside world, relations with suppliers should for the most part be limited to that department. Engineering or manufacturing personnel should not represent the company to outside suppliers except where their expertise is required and even then only by interfacing with the responsible purchaser. One of the industry's biggest problems is the engineering department's tendency to specify a particular vendor's product without the "or equal" phrase, or to specify a "special" when an off-the-shelf standard item will suffice. Such actions tend to foster the famous NIH (Not Invented Here) syndrome. (See Chapter 8 for a more detailed discussion of redesigning parts.)

ABC Stratification

The single most important step toward establishing an effective, cost-conscious purchasing department is the implementation of an ABC stratification system. While this vital concept will be detailed further in Chapter 7, the specific purchasing techniques soon to be discussed will probably not be effective if you do not understand and use ABC stratification or its equivalent as an overall operational premise.

Under an ABC stratification system, all materials and parts purchased by a company are classified into three groups. An "A" classification signals that the item is in the most expensive category. These parts are critical to the company's operation. The company will always want to know how many of these "A" items it has on hand. The buyers, the analysts, and the inventory control people—everyone involved in purchasing—should make it their business to know where the division stands with these items. "A" parts make up about 70 to 75 percent of the cost of all material, but they generally make up only 5 to 10 percent of the volume, or number, of parts. It is this "A" group that, when properly controlled, will lower costs and investment. Some people further subdivide this category into "A" and "AA" parts, with even greater control being exercised with the "AA" parts.

A "B" part is not as expensive as an "A" part, but is more expensive than a "C." This is the middle group of parts that make up about 20 percent of the number of parts that are used and approximately 20 percent of the dollars.

The "C" parts are the literal nuts and bolts of a company's operation—the bolts, the nuts, the screws, the washers—the low-dollar, standard, repetitive items that are used all the time. These items are inexpensive and can be bought in great volume once or twice a year. Because they represent 70 to 75 percent of the volume but only 5 to 10 percent of inventory investment, they can be heavily stocked with a minimum of control. Normally they represent 70 to 75 percent of the shortages.

By dividing all materials into these three categories, emphasis can be placed on the "A" parts. That is where the bulk of a company's money is; these are the items that require the most attention even though they make up only a small percentage of the total number of parts.

For "A" and "AA" parts, the purchasing department should be using blanket contracts and should be in close contact with the suppliers, potential suppliers, production schedule, and ability of these suppliers to meet the company's production requirements. In this way, the buyers will know if a supplier of an important "A" part is having any difficulty that could conceivably cause a delivery delay.

The purpose of ABC stratification is to place your resources on the most important items. By keeping careful track of "A" parts, an efficient inventory turn can be created. Large amounts of cash should not be tied up in expensive parts waiting idly to be placed into a finished product; nor should a purchasing department suddenly and unexpectedly be caught short without an expensive, hard-to-find "A" item. Cost reduction efforts in the purchasing area should concentrate on these "A" items. As with all purchasing techniques, organization, planning, control, and common sense are the keys.

One reason that a commitment to ABC stratification is so important is that the purchasing techniques discussed in the balance of this chapter will be most effective with these "A" parts.

Competition Is the Key

Competition is the key to any free enterprise system. Nowhere is this truer than in the purchasing area. Competition among suppliers should not be relegated to a bidding war. It should include a creative challenge to improve the products being purchased.

An open door policy, therefore, is the first golden rule of purchasing. Salespeople should know that the door to the purchasing department is always open to them. Management should emphasize that a purchasing agent cannot refuse to see a salesperson during working hours. Too many companies have rules limiting salespeoples' calls to particular days or hours. Our policy is to display a plaque in the lobby of every division's purchasing department reaffirming our policy (see Exhibit 6–2).

Exhibit 6–2   Open Door Policy

Dear Supplier:

At a time when it is becoming an increasingly common practice to restrict the days and hours that salespeople may call, we at Figgie International want you to know that you are welcome at any time or on any day that we conduct business. This is our policy.

We look to you for ideas, suggestions, and creative solutions that will enable us to reduce our costs and to offer the highest standards of quality and service to our customers. We don't think these things can or should be limited to particular days or hours.

As a sales-oriented company, we want you to know that our suppliers are always welcome. We appreciate your interest in our needs and we value your assistance and advice. Since quite a few of us in management came up through selling, we recognize that the salesperson's job is not an easy one and we don't intend to make it any harder than it is by establishing arbitrary restrictions.

We need you and we ask your help. We know you won't fail us, and if we fail to treat you fairly, please let me know personally. Thank you for coming in.

Sincerely yours,

Harry E. Figgie, Jr.
Chairman and Chief Executive Officer

It is not unusual for a purchasing department to fall into bad habits; for instance, to remain with one particular supplier because they've been doing business together for years. Just because a particular salesperson or vendor managed to furnish a product for the company

during a critical shortage period doesn't mean that supplier has necessarily remained competitive over the ensuing years.

Seekers of new business are coming into your shop too, and you can
stir up competition among them to your own benefit. When salespeople
are invited to bid and the bid is low on an item, they should be rewarded
with all or a portion of the business providing they are qualified vendors. All too often a purchasing agent will receive a lower set of prices
from a salesperson, only to turn around and ask the present supplier to
match the new prices. This is not the way the purchasing department
should be run. The fact that the new salesperson has broken the price at
the invitation of your purchasing department should earn that vendor at
least some of the business. Undue allegiance to one supplier will dis-
courage fresh suppliers from continuing to offer low bids, and reflects
negatively on the integrity of the purchasing department. The word passes quickly among vendors when procurement is not fairly or honestly
conducted.

One effective way to stimulate competition among suppliers is to display publicly a product board listing certain products that the company
purchases. Salespeople can see instantly where they stand on products
they are trying to sell, and on products they may not have thought of
trying to sell. Products on the board should be rotated periodically.
Design change suggestions and material substitution recommendations
will be forthcoming from suppliers, as well as potential price improvements.

An open door policy can have cost benefits over and above allowing
a purchasing department to locate the least expensive supplier. Recently a salesman, viewing a product board at one of our divisions, suggested substituting a plastic bolt for a metal one. Our buyer agreed to
the switch, which has resulted in an annual savings of many thousands
of dollars.

An open door policy makes a company accessible to new and innovative ideas. New techniques are being created every day. A company
should do its utmost to keep abreast of those that can save money. The
only way a company is going to be aware of these possibilities is to view
suppliers as experts in their particular fields, analyze what they have to
offer, and then make a decision as to whether it is appropriate for the
company's needs.

Avoiding Single-Sourced Items

A purchasing department always should try to avoid locking itself into one supplier. Again, competition is the name of the game. If for any reason one supplier submits what you consider to be an unreasonable price increase, you should, if at all possible, have an alternative supplier on standby. By following this advice, your company will never find itself in a sudden bind if a primary supplier experiences a strike, goes out of business, discontinues a particular item, or suffers a fire or other natural disaster.

Every effort should be made to obtain competitive quotations from various suppliers at least once a year; more often on "A" or "B" parts if cost increases do not appear justified. With the frequent and often dramatic price increases that have occurred during the past decade, a buyer must be able to determine what factors have increased the cost of items—labor, burden, raw material, packaging, transportation, or outside service costs, for example. Isolating various component costs helps to reconstruct the overall pricing structure. And remember, the "A" items should command special attention.

Standardization of Materials

Standardization of materials is an important, but often overlooked, cost-saving technique in the purchasing area. Whenever possible, the use of exotic or unusual materials should be avoided. Standard, common materials are less expensive both in the long and short term, and often one single part can be substituted for a wide range of hitherto diversified items without sacrificing efficiency, durability, or quality.

Whenever possible, purchasing departments should avoid engineering-sourced items. All too often the specifications given to a purchasing department are tied to an engineer's blueprints. If the design specifications for a concrete mixer, for example, call for a special, instead of a standard off-the-shelf cylinder, the purchasing department has no choice but to ask for bids for exactly such a cylinder, even if that means paying a higher price or accommodating a longer lead time. This kind of engineering-sourced item severely limits the negotiating position a purchaser ordinarily has with suppliers, and thus limits the ways in which the purchasing department can reduce costs.

One industry that has recognized and acted upon the principle of standardization is the steel industry, which no longer provides the same range of material, in terms of alloy content, size, thickness, and other specifications, as it once did. Steel manufacturers have realized that they can't be all things to all people. If a steel company does offer special, low-demand items, it either charges an extremely high price, or requires a very large minimum order, or both. Thus when a buyer insists on an exotic steel alloy, he or she has to pay dearly for it.

If, for example, blueprint specifications call for components of an assembly to be of various material types, thus resulting in buying small quantities of many different materials, it might be less expensive to standardize on the strongest material, paying more for material per pound but reducing overall costs due to volume reduction. Remember, we are concerned with reducing total costs, which may mean slight cost increases in some areas in order to save greater sums overall. Multiple orders, for example, even if less expensive per unit, will force the purchasing department to complete individual purchase orders, segregate the material, identify it, and handle it separately. All these bookkeeping and time consuming tasks cost money and increase the dangers of excess scrap and obsolescence.

Standardization must be instituted at the very outset of a product's design. In many companies, existing specifications do not coincide with the standardization that has taken place in the industry. For example, there are standard bolts and nuts—coarse and fine, various grades and threads—that are generally used throughout industry. In many cases, a buyer can take an existing set of blueprints and find a standard grade of bolt or cap screw that can be used throughout the entire application. This reduces the number of different parts to be used and increases the volume of the item to be purchased, thereby saving money. Unfortunately, this is an area in which engineers seem to prefer "specials" rather than the more common, standardized nuts, screws, bolts, and other "C" or low cost parts.

Negotiations with Suppliers

When a company is in need of a particular part, standard operating procedure is for the purchasing department to request bids from at least three or four different potential suppliers. These suppliers are sent a blueprint of the desired part, spelling out everything from design specifications, quantities required, type of material to be used, and the needed date of delivery. The purchasing department then receives a quotation from each supplier.

When the economic situation is relatively stable with inflation rates of 4 to 7 percent, there often is not a tremendous difference between the high and low price of any particular item. A low price might be 12¢ a pound, while the premium rate might be 12 1/2¢ or 13¢ a pound. However, in periods of rapid inflation or in other periods of unstable or high money costs, swings in prices can be as much as 30 to 50 percent. With supply reserves of many materials now limited and finite, these swings may well become the rule rather than the exception. We can expect material prices periodically to escalate rapidly in the years ahead.

Because of recent economic fluctuations, proper purchasing techniques are more vital than ever for the successful operation of a company. Inflation and shortages can drive up the price of some materials well in excess of the consumer or producer price indices. It is the purchasing department's job to combat this trend by breaking down the price structure and determining where costs can be cut or how price increases can be held down or rejected. Clearly, today's high cost of money is also a reason why it is so important that a purchasing department do all it can to help keep inventory levels to a minimum without causing undue stockouts or clerical costs.

Obviously, at least some idea of comparative pricing must be maintained. At the very least, the purchasing department should know why they are using its present suppliers. It may be paying slightly more for an item, for example, but the material may be delivered in such a way that overall costs are actually less.

Whatever the reason for doing business with a particular supplier, a company president can partially assess the quality of the purchasing department by determining whether for every purchased item a second and third source was rejected in favor of the primary source. If the purchasing department is sourcing its material from a supplier because "that's the way we've always done it," or because "it's worked well in the past," you can immediately assume that there is something fundamentally wrong with the way that department is operating. The same holds true if the same vendors are sourced time after time. Any purchasing agent can protect chosen vendors for long periods. Rotation of bidders is necessary in order to make certain that your current supplier is the best in terms of both cost and quality. Personal knowledge on the part of the company head will help ascertain whether the purchasing department is on its toes.

When I was a young sales engineer, I learned many lessons which have remained with me, but one in particular stands out in my mind. I received an order for 500,000 cap screws per month. A second division of the same large company sought a bid for 50,000 per month for the identical part. We priced this second order on a strictly incremental basis, without factoring in the cost of setup or teardown. It was extra business, so we priced it accordingly. We lost the second, smaller bid. Someone in a "garage shop" who knew much less about pricing analysis than we did had offered a much lower bid.

The lesson: Any price can be beaten. In both cases the purchasers were highly qualified divisions of one of the country's largest companies. Their philosophies were obviously different. The larger division emphasized quality, ability to deliver, staying power, financial stability, and the ability to deliver to blueprint. The smaller division made its decision solely on price.

The point of this story is that you must make your own policy perfectly clear to your procurement people so that they know what to look for when purchasing. While the general rule that price, quality and service should all be emphasized is a good one, it must be recognized that there will be some instances where a purchasing department will be asked for a product at the best available price regardless of quality and service. Other times they will be asked to emphasize quality and/or service over price.

Back when I was working in the screw machine products industry, the head of the association gave me an interesting piece of information that provided further insight into the natural desire to offer the lowest price in order to win a contract. At the time there was a 10 to 15 percent company turnover in this industry each year, and according to the head of the industry association this had been occurring at the same rate for a number of years. The number of machines, however, remained constant. This meant that when one small company failed, another person bought the machinery and tried his hand. Clearly, this 10 to 15 percent of the companies did not have an adequate understanding of their costs, but they offered great prices for the short periods of time they remained in business. This is something to keep in mind during our discussion in Chapter 10 of the tremendous importance of proper pricing techniques.

Whenever possible, a purchasing department should try to do business with one vendor for a variety of products. This saves administrative costs, is more practical in terms of developing a rapport with the supplier, and allows the purchaser more room for negotiation. The purchasing department should also stress vendor stocking. Let vendors pay to inventory the material; it is frequently to their advantage because they can get longer, more efficient run lengths. With some type of guaranteed use over a blanket period the vendor is protected. From your company's point of view, if an item can be shipped periodically, it results in a faster turnover and less inventory investment. When interest costs are high, this becomes even more of a key factor. This is graphically demonstrated in Chapter 7's "sawtooth" graph (Exhibit 7-6).

The three most important criteria for a purchasing agent to remember when choosing a supplier are price, applicable quality, and adequate service. In addition, however, there are always countless other variables. It is up to the individual buyer to use experience, common sense, and imagination to continually come up with ways in which material costs can be reduced. Some of the key areas that must be considered are:

1. Price

2. Distance from supplier to plant

3. Reliability of delivery

4. Special factors affecting bids

5. Size of order

6. Stability and reliability of suppliers

7. Supplier's creative contributions

8. Quality

All these variables have to be weighed by a purchasing agent who can juggle the entire range of possible solutions before coming up with the best price as balanced against the best-suited product and most reliable supplier.

For example, the lowest-priced supplier might be located in a distant city and therefore have higher transportation costs or an unacceptable delivery date. Another supplier may be offering a particularly low price, but only for a minimum run of 300 pieces. This doesn't do you much good if you only need 200. In yet another case, you might happen to know of a supplier who just after giving you a quote lost a large order. This supplier may be willing to lower his bid now that his factories require work. Or maybe the best price can be obtained by agreeing to have your own truck pick up the pieces from a supplier who had a very low bid but very high delivery costs.

There are, in other words, a limitless number of possibilities and factors that a good purchasing agent must consider before signing a contract with a supplier. (See Exhibits 6–3 through 6–7.)

Once a buyer has decided to do business with a particular supplier, and when a general, ballpark price has been agreed upon, the purchasing department should not necessarily accept the quoted price. The philosophy, as stated previously, of everyone from the company president down to the most junior buyer, should be that costs can always be reduced.

If, for example, a purchasing department accepts multiple quotes on an item and vendor A comes in at $1 and everyone else comes in at $1.10, the assumption still must be that there is fat even in the $1 figure. The purchasing staff should sit down with vendor A, with the understanding that they want to do business, but that they also want to find ways in which the $1 figure can be reduced. This is the time when a buyer's experience and expertise come into play.

Packaging and Shipping

Packaging and shipping are two of the simplest areas in which cost saving measures can be implemented. A glance at a package of ball bearings, for example, might tell a purchaser that the packaging is unnecessarily complex, that it is triple wall corrugated when it could just as effectively be single wall corrugated, or that it is being packaged in a crate instead of an inexpensive container. (See Exhibit 6–7.)

Exhibit 6–3 Negotiation Example 1

One supplier can guarantee an early delivery date, but is $5 higher per item than the lowest bid received. A phone call indicates that this supplier's costs are high because of being forced, for whatever reason, to pay an exorbitant rate for the relatively small amounts of steel required for the particular item. The buyer may be in a position to provide the steel from the company's own inventory, or perhaps the buyer simply knows where it can be purchased inexpensively. Or discussions with the company's engineering and factory people may identify a more standardized steel that is readily available at a much lower cost. The buyer, by telling the supplier to quote the job excluding the steel, will in this way find the path to the lowest price.

Exhibit 6–4 Negotiation Example 2

The purchasing department and vendor A sit down to discuss ways in which costs can be cut on a $1 item. First, it is determined that shipping the item ten to a carton instead of six will immediately reduce the cost by 2¢. Next, through further investigation, the buyer learns that the aluminum required had been ordered to outdated specifications and that the current standard for this item is a better quality, but less expensive grade aluminum. This reduces the cost per item by another 4¢. Then the purchasing department asks the supplier why transportation costs were estimated at 10¢, and the answer is unsatisfactory. The purchasing department can arrange for a company-owned truck to deliver the goods just as well. (Or maybe transportation costs are not included, but the purchaser tells the supplier that the $1 figure, which has been knocked down to 94¢, is acceptable only if the cost includes delivery. The supplier may agree, even if he had never previously considered the question.)

Now the purchasing department can buy the same item but at 84¢ per unit [$1 − (2¢ + 4¢ + 10¢)]. At least most of this 16¢ savings will go right to the company, since the cost of the company-owned truck will be nowhere near as expensive as 10¢ per unit. It may even be that the truck is presently returning from another job empty, in which case there will be virtually no additional cost. Total costs, therefore, will have been reduced by 16 percent.

Exhibit 6–5   Negotiation Example 3

A company uses 4,000 pieces of a particular item annually. In the past, the company had always ordered 1,000 pieces every three months. The purchasing department, however, at the urging of its new company president, sits down with the supplier and learns that 1,000 pieces cost $5 each, plus setup costs of $1,000, which include the tooling and fixturing that have to be brought into the line only for as long as it takes to fill this order. The setup costs, however, will be $1,000 whether the order is for 1,000 pieces or 4,000 pieces. The vendor agrees to run the full year's requirements and store them, shipping to the company in periodic partial quantities. The purchasing department then must negotiate to keep at least most of the $3,000 savings for the company rather than allow it to go to the vendor.

Exhibit 6–6   Negotiation Example 4

A vendor's peak season is January through March. From April to June he tends to lay people off. A purchasing department agrees to give this supplier an order in May, with the understanding that the supplier will have to warehouse the material until it is needed. By committing early for an order with a cyclical supplier, a purchasing department can often reduce the supplier's total costs, a savings that in turn can be passed on to the purchaser.

Exhibit 6–7   Negotiation Example 5

A manufacture of golf balls packages them in three sleeve containers and then packs them four sleeves to a box with a filler. The box, in other words, is too large for the four sleeves so a filler is needed to occupy the excess space. A new purchasing agent comes in and, after making certain that marketing agrees that a smaller package will not detract from the salability of the product, shrinks the box, eliminating the need for a filler. Costs are reduced by eliminating unnecessary material, as well as by making the total product lighter and less bulky, and therefore less expensive to transport.

During the 1980s, deregulation of transportation has added another ingredient to the purchasing department's ability to negotiate price. When transportation costs were fixed by the government there was not much the purchasing department could do to reduce costs. Today, however, with the high price of fuel, lowering transportation costs can be an extremely important component of any overall cost-cutting effort. Again, competition is the name of the game. Only when there is competition does a purchasing department have a variety of cost-cutting options.

One tip-off that a purchasing department is not doing its job properly is when a purchase order does not specify routing instructions. If the buyer's instructions to a supplier are to ship the applicable item "best way," or if there are no instructions at all, that item, nine times out of ten, is not going to be transported by the least expensive means. It is the buyer's job, not the supplier's, to make certain that all costs from production through delivery are as low as possible.

Integrity of Buyers

Because the bulk of the sales dollar revolves around the purchasing department, and because the best way to reduce material costs is to allow buyers the freedom to negotiate, this is also, unfortunately, the area that produces the greatest temptation to commit acts of omission or commission. Make certain that every member of your purchasing department is beyond reproach.

It is the responsibility of the division or company president to make it perfectly clear to all concerned that gifts and gratuities have no place in the ethical business transactions between buyer and seller. This theme should be strongly emphasized by any corporate procurement office. At Figgie International, it is the responsibility of the director of purchasing each year to see that all our divisions send out letters to their suppliers reaffirming this policy.

There are certain purchasing areas that seem particularly susceptible. A key responsibility of the purchasing department, in addition to procurement, is to sell scrap, obsolete, or excess material. In order to maximize the return to the corporation, you should make every effort to make certain this is done in an objective and comprehensive manner. These tasks require knowledge the purchasing department generally does not have. Do not allow this task to be performed in a perfunctory manner. The person selected to perform such a function should get the help and expertise necessary to maximize the return from these kinds of sales.

Long-Term Goals

While it is rare that an important, long-term strategic decision is made on a unilateral basis by the purchasing department, there are five long-term management functions in which the purchasing department should play an important role. They are:

1. Product redesign

2. Value analysis

3. Make-or-buy decisions

4. Pricing

5. Forecasting

   Product redesign, value analysis, and make-or-buy decisions are all discussed in Chapter 8, while Chapter 10 is devoted entirely to pricing. Chapter 9 concerns itself with sales forecasting, although a brief preview of the importance of forecasting, particularly how it relates to the purchasing department, follows.

Forecasting

Due to the fact that purchasing agents have contacts with the outside vendor world, by the very nature of the job, they have access to what is happening in the marketplace. They are, therefore, in many ways in the best position to provide information to the rest of the company as to future fluctuations in the price and availability of the raw materials instrumental to the company's operations. The need for a company's purchasing department to keep abreast of trends and to maintain a close and trusting relationship with suppliers has always been apparent. Recent shortages of raw materials have made this requirement even more vital. In the near future, and probably for evermore, various types of materials will become increasingly difficult to obtain. Copper, bauxite, tungsten, oil, molybdenum, and chromium are only a few examples of items that will have to be followed closely.

Many companies, my own included, are not in a position in the marketplace to establish or foresee every trend in usage, consumption, and availability that might affect them. But because of the volatile state of the economy, and because such a large percentage of many raw materials must be imported, shortages are bound to occur and prices are apt to rise astronomically, often in a very short period of time. If it is not silver or gold or oil, it will be something else. This kind of situation will, at the very least, prevent many of the smaller suppliers from maintaining the inventories necessary to meet the immediate demands of all companies. From the point of view of suppliers, the cost of money will create a situation in which they simply will not have the capital to properly protect their sources. Concurrent with this is the problem of keeping inventories low, while at the same time recognizing that quick business recovery spurts can create sudden shortages and make the resulting long lead times a luxury a purchasing department cannot afford. This just adds to the importance of accurate forecasting and knowing where you are in the business cycle (see Chapter 9).

All these circumstances point to the possibility of many small suppliers going out of business, leaving relatively few sources for many vital materials. This means that companies will have to deal with fewer suppliers more and more frequently, increasing the importance of creating and maintaining a close relationship between buyer and seller. You must develop a rapport with suppliers so that they are aware of your demands and so that they, because of your reliability, will continue to service your account even when shortages do occur. This does not mean, however, that price consciousness should be surrendered.

Some of the techniques the Japanese are using in multiple year procurement bear further investigation in the future. To take advantage of them, however, one has to be well locked down on design, and be able to ascertain accurately at least minimum forecasts.

Summary

The importance of purchasing should depend to a large extent on the percentage that raw materials and purchased parts represents to your sales dollar. For most companies material ranks as the largest cost, yet the purchasing department is not given its proper emphasis. As a result, companies and divisions lose profits unnecessarily through lack of understanding, slipshod practices, neglect, and lack of proper information and planning. Sourcing and resourcing and negotiation and renegotiation must become, if they are not already, constant and continuous programs with an emphasis on "A" parts.

The ever-changing economic situation, the finite quantities of certain raw materials, and the unending supply of new parts, products, and technologies make it vital for purchasing personnel to be highly qualified, alert, and have direct communication with the company head and key department heads.

My experience indicates that to accomplish all this there are at least two hurdles that must be surmounted. The first is the education of the company head so that he or she can properly direct and evaluate the purchasing manager and coordinate purchasing efforts with engineering and manufacturing, not to mention sales.

The second hurdle is to eliminate the feeling that purchasing is a dead-end by rotating promising young personnel through several departments such as purchasing, cost accounting, industrial engineering, and quality control. Outside training and membership in the Purchasing Management Association is an added dimension that is also desirable.

Always remember that it is unlikely that any area within your company has more to offer in the effort to reduce costs than the purchasing department. And no area is more often overlooked.

The following chapter continues to concentrate on how material costs can be cut. Two of the most effective tools, ABC inventory control and the economic order quantity, are discussed in detail.

7

ABC Inventory Control

In Chapter 6, the classification of parts through an ABC inventory control system was briefly outlined as part of an overall, comprehensive strategy to reduce costs in the purchasing area. ABC classification is perhaps the single most important technique that a purchasing department can use to place itself in a position to cut costs.

This chapter, therefore, will be devoted to a further discussion of the ABC system, as well as the economic order quantity (EOQ), a technique used to equate the comparative cost of carrying an item in inventory to the cost of obtaining it from an outside source or manufacturing it.

ABC inventory is a statistical method of dividing up inventory. Quite simply, experience has taught that given a reasonable universe of parts:

- 5 to 10 percent of your parts will represent 70 to 75 percent of your cost but only 5 to 10 percent of your shortages ("A" parts).

- 20 percent of your parts will represent 20 percent of your cost and 20 percent of your shortages ("B" parts).

- 70 to 75 percent of your parts will represent 5 to 10 percent of your cost and 70 to 75 percent of your shortages ("C" parts).

This means that in order to save money, reduce obsolescence, and turn your inventory faster, you should source, negotiate, control, cost redesign, and otherwise concentrate your efforts on 5 to 30 percent of your parts ("A"s and "B"s). The other 70 to 75 percent can be bought in large quantities with a minimum of inventory controls since both the investment and obsolescence will be relatively small. Such a program should materially reduce shortages, as will be discussed shortly.

I once reduced a truck to all its basic parts. The results shown in Exhibit 7–1 may surprise you, but they represent a typical ABC distribution.

The First Step

Many presidents and chief executive officers of small to medium size companies are unfamiliar with the ABC system and therefore do not know where to begin even if they are convinced of the system's tremendous value. By the same token, it does little good for the company head to ask the purchasing chief whether they are following the many cost-saving procedures described in Chapter 6 if the president lacks the background, expertise or experience necessary to determine the accuracy of the purchaser's response.

The simplest, most effective initial step for a president or chief executive officer who is unfamiliar with the ABC system is to understand the 80–20 rule, and then immediately take advantage of this rule for the particular company in question. Twenty percent of a company's finished items typically provide 80 percent of sales. As the company's head of operations, you should begin by learning the identity of this 20 percent of the company's products. In turn, within this 20 percent, you should learn which components make up 80 percent of their cost. These are the parts that should receive attention first and foremost because these are the parts that are making up the largest share of the company's material costs.

Armed with this information, which is really only a shorthand method for identifying a company's "A" parts, you can then sit down with the persons in charge of your purchasing, engineering and manufacturing departments to determine ways in which these parts can be purchased and inventoried more effectively. Redesign discussions can be held simultaneously.

Exhibit 7–1 Profile of ABC

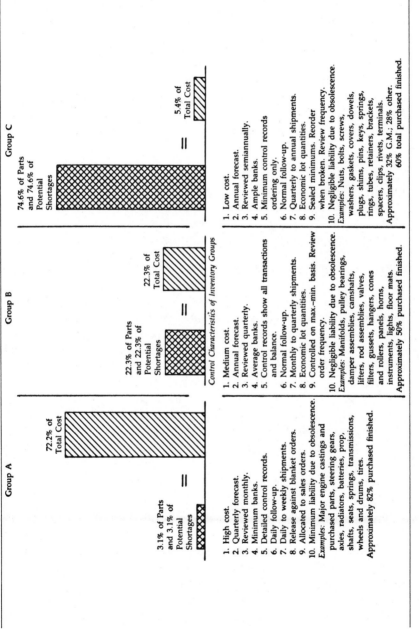

Group A	Group B	Group C
3.1% of Parts and 3.1% of Potential Shortages = 72.2% of Total Cost	22.3% of Parts and 22.3% of Potential Shortages = 22.3% of Total Cost	74.6% of Parts and 74.6% of Potential Shortages = 5.4% of Total Cost

Control Characteristics of Inventory Groups

Group A

1. High cost.
2. Quarterly forecast.
3. Reviewed monthly.
4. Minimum banks.
5. Detailed control records.
6. Daily follow-up.
7. Daily to weekly shipments.
8. Release against blanket orders.
9. Allocated to sales orders.
10. Minimum liability due to obsolescence.

Examples: Major engine castings and purchased parts, steering gears, axles, radiators, batteries, prop, shafts, seats, springs, transmissions, wheels and drums, tires.

Approximately 82% purchased finished.

Group B

1. Medium cost.
2. Annual forecast.
3. Reviewed quarterly.
4. Average banks.
5. Control records show all transactions and balance.
6. Normal follow-up.
7. Monthly to quarterly shipments.
8. Economic lot quantities.
9. Controlled on max.–min. basis. Review order frequency.
10. Negligible liability due to obsolescence.

Examples: Manifolds, pulley bearings, damper assemblies, camshafts, lifters, rod assemblies, valves, filters, gussets, hangers, cones and rollers, panels, horns, instruments, lights, floor mats.

Approximately 50% purchased finished.

Group C

1. Low cost.
2. Annual forecast.
3. Reviewed semiannually.
4. Ample banks.
5. Minimum control records ordering only.
6. Normal follow-up.
7. Quarterly to annual shipments.
8. Economic lot quantities.
9. Sealed minimums. Reorder when broken. Review frequency.
10. Negligible liability due to obsolescence.

Examples: Nuts, bolts, screws, washers, gaskets, covers, dowels, plugs, shims, pins, keys, springs, rings, tubes, retainers, brackets, spacers, clips, rivets, terminals.

Approximately 32% G.M.; 28% other. 60% total purchased finished.

This is obviously only an initial shortcut to implementing an ABC system, but it will allow a company to obtain impressive results immediately. The next step of course is to classify all component parts into "A"s and "B"s and "C"s and to undertake the more sophisticated techniques described in the remainder of this chapter. But for even this initial step to be successful, it is absolutely vital for you, as the top executive of a manufacturing company, to know enough about sourcing so that you can understand and evaluate the information you receive from department heads, the purchasing chief in particular.

Implementing an ABC System

Before detailing the benefits of ABC inventory control, it is important to make clear that an ABC classification system is only one technique used to classify raw material and component parts. (It can also be used for sales.) I happen to believe it is the best technique for most situations, but there are others. Regardless of what classification method is used, the goal should always be to divide material and parts in such a way that those relatively few items that represent the highest cost and generally the highest investment ("A" parts) are not the ones left sitting idly in inventory and are not out of stock for their full lead time. Conversely, the many low-cost items ("C" parts) should be purchased infrequently, since no matter how many of them a company has on hand, these parts will not tie up large sums of money. Of equal importance is that these low-cost items tend to cause the greatest shortages. Infrequent, large purchases of "C" parts should eliminate the bulk of stock outages (as will be discussed later) and still represent only a very small portion of total inventory investment.

Translating this theory into an actual operation is really quite simple. If a company with $10 million in sales purchases 75,000 1/4¢ screws six times a year, the money saved in inventory will not nearly make up for the added cost in filing the paperwork every other month, to say nothing of the serious risk of frequently depleting inventory, thereby causing shortages and stockouts. Rather, a company's purchasing department should be expending its energies on the more expensive parts—the parts which when properly purchased and controlled can result in major savings.

In my experience, the best way to ensure such a division of parts is through ABC inventory control. ABC is not difficult to implement and it can be maintained with relatively little effort since records actually have to be kept for only 20 to 30 percent of your parts. Most important, the system works, bringing quick and beneficial results.

The initial step in ABC inventory control is to separate all of the component parts in every product being manufactured, and classify each part according to its cost, irrespective of whether that part is made or bought. The classified parts should then be divided into three groups: "A," "B," and "C." The most expensive parts should be listed in the "A" group, and the medium-priced items in the "B" group. Into the "C" group, therefore, should go all of the remaining, relatively inexpensive, component parts. The cost of each part should be listed within each of the three groups. This classification of parts must be made for each finished product that is produced. The exception to this rule is for "specials" or items that are used infrequently. These items are treated separately, in effect as a fourth classification.

Although cogent arguments can be made for using either the unit or the total volume system of ABC, I believe that when determining if a part is an "A," "B," or "C" part, unit value, rather than total value, should be used. For example, if a company uses one million screws at 2¢ each, each screw should be classified as a "C" part despite the fact that the company is spending a total of $20,000 for them. I have found total value to be useful only when the same parts are used day after day on an assembly line where relatively few finished models or products are made. Unit value, on the other hand, works in all cases, has a much broader range of usage, and gives maximum protection against stock outage of the "C" parts.

By studying Exhibit 7-2, one can begin to understand the form and substance of ABC inventory control. Note that there are 231 parts costing less than 5¢ and 315 parts that cost between 5¢ and 10¢. Out of the 1215 separate component parts used in the production of this model, 546 parts cost 10¢ or less and 849 cost $1 or less.

Most significant is the fact that only 119 parts cost more than $25. These, then, are the "A" parts. There are 247 parts in the "B" group, costing from $1 to $25. There are 849 "C" parts, costing from less than 1¢ to $1. Exhibit 7-2, which is an actual example, clearly demonstrates that even in a model costing many thousands of dollars, the great bulk of its component parts have relatively low unit values.

Exhibit 7-2 Breakdown of Parts by Cost

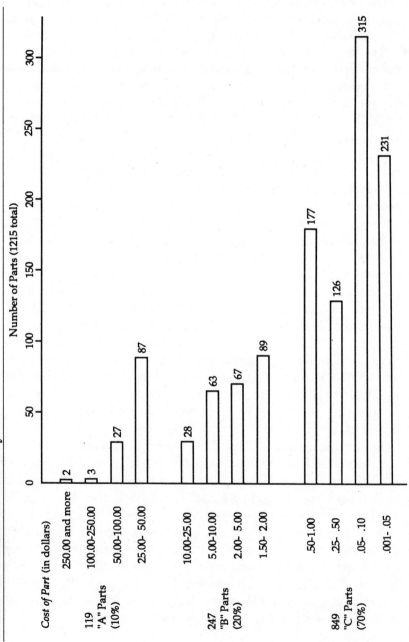

For this particular model, the "C" parts make up 70 percent of the total number of parts, the "B" parts make up 20 percent, and the "A" parts only 10 percent. This is a typical and reasonable ratio throughout most manufacturing operations.

Further analysis of Exhibit 7–2 reveals that while the "C" parts make up a large percentage of the total *volume* of parts, they make up a very small percentage of total material costs. In fact, Exhibit 7–3, by taking the median dollar figure for each category (the $.05 to $.10 category, in other words, is computed at $.075), demonstrates that in this particular model the "C" parts make up only about 3 percent of total material costs.

Exhibit 7–3 Cost Breakdown of A, B, and C Parts

"A" Parts		"B" Parts		"C" Parts	
No. of Parts	Median Cost of Parts ($)	No. of Parts	Median Cost of Parts ($)	No. of Parts	Median Cost of Parts ($)
87 × 37.5	= $3,262	89 × 1.75	= $ 156	231 × .01	= $ 2.31
27 × 75	= $2,025	67 × 3.5	= $ 234	315 × .075	= $ 23.62
3 × 175	= $ 525	63 × 7.5	= $ 472	126 × .38	= $ 47.88
2 × 300	= $ 600	28 × 17.5	= $ 490	177 × .75	= $132.75
	$6,412		$1,352		$207

Total cost of all parts = $7,971
Total cost of "A" parts = $6,412 (80%)
Total cost of "B" parts = $1,352 (17%)
Total cost of "C" parts = $ 207 (3%)

Variations within the ABC Method

It should be noted that a breakdown of parts into an ABC classification will not look the same for any two products. Some items will be made up of more expensive parts than others, so the cutoff need not necessarily be $1 for "C" parts or $25 for "B" parts as in Exhibits 7–2 and 7–3. For example, a $1 part could be classified as a "B" part or a $5 part as an "A." These details will depend on the makeup of the individual items in question. In addition, "C" parts normally should comprise more than the 3 percent costs that they did in Exhibit 7–3. Rarely, however, should "C" parts exceed 10 percent of costs, so the theories demonstrated by our examples will be valid in most instances. Remember, a good rule of thumb is that 5 to 10 percent of your items will make up 70 to 75 percent of your costs, 20 percent of your items will make up 20 percent of your costs, and 70 to 75 percent of your items will make up 5 to 10 percent of your costs.

In some classification systems, "B" parts are eliminated altogether, and a distinction is made between "A" and "C" parts only. Other companies have a special "A +" or "AA" category for a few very expensive parts. As with virtually all the cost reduction techniques described in this text the purpose is to enable you—the chief executive, president, general manager, or other top-level manager—to understand basic concepts so that you will recognize the importance of implementing these cost reduction techniques as part of a comprehensive program to improve profits. You can then hire experts to implement them, or train your people, or both.

Reducing Shortages

In addition to improving inventory turn which frees working capital, transfers it into cash, and reduces costs by lowering interest expenses and obsolescence, another primary purpose of an ABC system is to minimize stock runouts and to maximize the speed with which a stockout can be rectified. It should be noted, however, that regardless of your safety stock, stockouts can never be fully eliminated. This can be proven statistically since, as demonstrated clearly by Exhibit 7–4, when the level of safety stock increases, the probability line becomes asymptotic.

The probability of stock runouts varies per item and per product. Rates are generally based upon forecast variances and volatility of usage. For example, in Exhibit 7–5 there are 12 truck models classified

Exhibit 7-4 Stockout Rate Graph

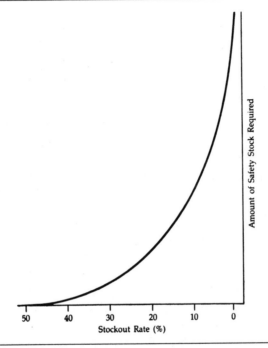

into 8 categories. Notice that each category has a different rate of probable runout versus forecast demand. If we provide a 40 percent safety stock for the type 20 model, the chance of runout is only 4 percent. If, on the other hand, the same level is provided for model 22, the chance rises to 21 percent.

What is really called for here is a combination of judgment, statistical evaluation, and analysis of the cost of extra inventory. There are, however, ways to minimize both the runout risk and investment. They will be discussed toward the end of this chapter.

Keeping this discussion of stockouts in mind, let us now progress to a better understanding of what is called the "order point principle" by taking a look at Exhibit 7–6, the "sawtooth chart."

Exhibit 7–6 demonstrates that over a two-and-a-half-month period, with a monthly usage of 100, 250 of this part will be used with a reserve (safety stock) of 50. However, in order to maintain an adequate amount of this part it would have to be reordered two months before it was actually needed. This is referred to as the order (or replacement) lead time.

Exhibit 7-5 Stock Run-out Probabilities

Inventory Level (% of Forecast Demand)	Probability of Run-out[1] Models							
	20	22	22R	50	23D	120–122	226–406	236, 236D, 536
100	50%	65%	55%	50%	58%	63%	66%	45%
105	40	59	47	44	53	55	60	41
110	34	53	39	38	47	49	55	38
115	25	47	31	33	42	42	50	35
120	20	41	24	29	37	35	45	31
125	14	35	18	24	32	29	40	28
130	10	30	13	20	27	23	36	25
135	6	25	10	16	23	18	31	23
140	4	21	6	13	19	13	28	20
145	2	17	4	10	15	10	24	18
150		13	3	8	13	8	20	16
155		10	2	6	10	5	18	14
160		8		4	8	4	14	12
165		6		3	6	2	12	10
170		4		2	4		10	8
175		3			3		8	6
180		2			2		6	5
185							5	4
190							4	3
195							3	2
200								

[1]All these models are different trucks.

Exhibit 7–6 Sawtooth Chart

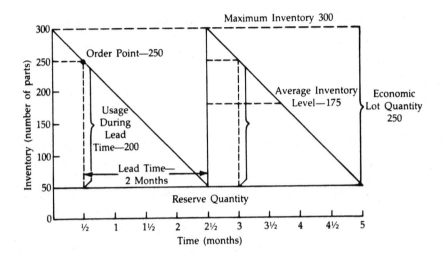

The theory is that on the day you run out, a new quantity of 250 is received from your vendor. If there is a delay, your reserve quantity in this example will protect you for an average of two weeks.

Your average inventory is 175 (250 ÷ 2 + 50), assuming your economic order quantity is 250 pieces and your reserve is 50 pieces. (This particular item would probably be a "B" part.)

In order to understand the real advantages of ABC inventory, keep your eye on the sawtooth chart and imagine two scenarios—first an "A" part, and then a "C" part.

Assume we use 100 per month and receive our "A" parts once every month—12 times a year. If there were no safety stock we'd go from 100 to 0 every month for a twenty-four-times inventory turn (annual usage of 1,200 divided by average monthly inventory of 50). Even with the same 50-unit safety stock, our average inventory would drop to 100

(100 ÷ 2 + 50), from the 175 that we showed over the two-and-a-half-month period. You can see we'd have a much lower investment since, as was noted earlier, "A" parts make up approximately 75 percent of investment. If you do run short on an "A" part and deplete your safety stock, you know you'll still be getting a new shipment sometime within the month, and you won't have to wait the full order lead time, which is generally quite long for "A" parts. This means that customers will not be kept waiting for long.

Now imagine a "C" part. In this case, a year's quantity should be ordered. Go back to the sawtooth graph and imagine that the 300 becomes 3,000 and the two and a half months becomes one year. For eleven months the "C" part is its own safety stock, and the average inventory is 1,550 (3,000 ÷ 2 + 50). During this eleven-twelfths of the year there is almost no chance that a runout will occur. Only during the twelfth month, once a year, will a runout be possible. Even if such an emergency does occur, the "C" part is generally easily replaced because it is often a stock item such as a nut, screw, washer, or other common, standard part. Remember, "C" parts represent only 5 to 10 percent of inventory costs but 70 to 75 percent of shortages. Even if a year's quantity is ordered, you will still have a two times turn. "A" parts, on the other hand, should be turned twenty-four times or even twelve times, while "B" parts fall in between the two extremes.

Viewing the situation practically, it should be apparent that a manufacturer can afford to purchase large quantities of "C" parts infrequently. These can be inventoried without tying up large sums of money, and buying in bulk will permit the purchasing department to make the best possible low-cost buy. When "C" parts are stocked sufficiently, and a reliable control and delivery schedule is implemented for "B" parts, the purchasing department, as discussed earlier, can appropriately concentrate on the handling, control, and turnover of the expensive "A" and "AA" parts. Sometimes you need only operate an "A–C" system, dividing "B" items into the other two categories.

A properly administered ABC system reduces record keeping, the expediting, the rush, the extra setups and teardowns. It increases your inventory turn, releases capital, reduces obsolescence, and permits purchasing to make long-range buys at the best negotiated prices. It permits them to concentrate on the more expensive "A" and "B" parts, issuing blanket contracts and scheduling the parts periodically.

Three Steps for ABC Control

Although inflexible rules should not be laid down, certain pragmatic steps do suggest themselves for effective utilization of the three basic elements of ABC control. For "A" and "AA" parts, for example, inventories should of course be kept to a minimum. Tight controls should be kept, along with daily, detailed records. Purchase blanket orders, have your vendor keep an inventory of them, and schedule them into your plant frequently. If they arrive in monthly quantities twelve times a year, the turnover theoretically is twenty-four times annually for 70 percent of your investment. These parts should remain in work-in-process the shortest time possible in order to hasten overall inventory turn.

For "B" parts, a modified program should be implemented, combining the characteristics of control exercised for "A" and "C" parts. As noted earlier, however, in certain instances some of these items listed as "B" parts might be categorized as "C" parts, or even as "A" parts. The need for "B" parts should be anticipated in an annual forecast which should be reviewed quarterly in a check against usage of inventory. Banks of inventories should be maintained at "average" levels—not too high, not too low—and control records should show all transactions (in and out), plus the balance in inventory. Normal follow-up will suffice.

Shipments of the "B" items should be ordered on a monthly to quarterly basis, the latter if possible, and the purchasing department should try to buy them in economic quantity lots. The order frequency should be reviewed periodically. Some will lend themselves to blanket orders with periodic releases for shipment.

"C" items cause the greatest number of shortages and exact wasteful cost in time and energy unless adequate provisions are made. To avoid these problems, buy "C" items in quantity. It will do no harm to be "up to your ears" in these parts, and by ordering in bulk the purchasing department will be dealing with its supplier from a position of strength, allowing negotiations for the lowest possible price. If you bring "C" parts in once a year, theoretically your turnover will be twice a year for 5 to 10 percent of your investment. If the parts are received twice a year, the theoretical turnover is four times, an equally acceptable turn for "C" parts.

The purchase of "C" parts can be made from an annual forecast which should be reviewed no more often than semiannually. Minimum records, for the purpose of ordering only, should be kept. Remember also that obsolescence goes hand in hand with investment. By controlling "A" and "B" parts closely, the cost of obsolescence will be minimized. Obsoleting "C" parts is 3 percent of 5 to 10 percent, or .15 to .3 percent of your total inventory investment. This will not cause a problem. In addition, these tend to be standard items which your vendor will frequently take back at a slight discount.

The paperwork for these "C" parts is minimal. A large economic order quantity of, say, a certain type of cap screw, is received at the company dock, and the bulk of the order is subsequently delivered to the assembly floor. A predetermined safety quantity simultaneously is bagged and tagged and placed in an easily accessible storage area. When all the cap screws on the assembly floor are used up, the safety bag is retrieved and sent to the assembly floor. The ticket attached to the safety bag is pulled off, dropped into a box, and immediately sent to the purchasing department for reordering.

Prior to the computer age, an ABC system could be installed extremely inexpensively with two to three clerical employees posting the "A"s and "B"s with a simple card file system. This is an area where the computer has tended to hurt rather than help by complicating a simple process and expanding controls unnecessarily to the "C" parts.

Many company presidents, when told of the importance of classifying component parts, will argue that theirs is a 40,000-part company and it is impossible to keep track of 40,000 individual parts. (For some reason that I can never understand, 40,000 seems to be the magic number.) It is true that 40,000 parts can stretch the limits of a hand-controlled system. Even if the effort were successful, the operation might not be cost effective. This is the advantage of the ABC system. In a 40,000-part company, only 4,000 parts will be "A" parts needing the most attention, and only 8,000 will be "B" parts needing moderate attention. The remaining 28,000 parts will be "C"s requiring no posting records at all. Hence, a 40,000-part system really becomes a 10,000- to 12,000-part system, which is easily handled by two or three clerks posting a card file system. Although they are easily adaptable to computers, don't make the mistake of keeping records on the 28,000 "C" parts.

All that is necessary for this system to work properly is the most basic manufacturing discipline. The worker who opens the safety bag must pull off the ticket and drop it into a box, the ticket then must be sent to the purchasing department, which in turn must know how long the safety quantity will last and therefore how quickly another large quantity will be needed. They should only have to make this buy once, or no more than twice, a year. A calculated EOQ will suggest to them the amount that should be purchased. The entire process is easily handled with a traveling requisition which, while simple, contains all necessary data for this process.

Should a standard "C" part stockout, it generally can be replaced quickly from a nearby supply house, thereby minimizing any disruption until a new regular shipment arrives. As was demonstrated in the sawtooth chart, this should only occur once a year at most on a "C" part.

The Savings

Now let's take a look at precisely what kind of savings can be expected through the implementation of an ABC program. This time we will use as an example an ABC classification where "A" parts make up 5 percent of the total number of parts and 75 percent of total cost; "B" parts are 20 percent by volume and 20 percent by cost; and "C" parts 75 percent by volume and 5 percent by cost. Remember, without controls shortages can on average be expected to correspond to the share of the whole that the item represents. In other words, if "A" parts make up 5 percent of the total number of parts, they can be expected to make up about 5 percent of the shortages. "C" parts on the other hand, make up 70 to 75 percent of the shortages.

In Exhibit 7-7 there is a normal monthly requirement for $1,000,000 worth of inventory. This is the total amount required for parts that are being processed through the shop. With an average 3.5 months of inventory the average investment is $3.5 million, from which is subtracted a 5 percent obsolescence factor or, in dollars, $171,428. The average usable investment is thus $3,428,571.

By applying the ABC method to this same inventory requirement, the results are quite different, as is demonstrated by Exhibit 7–7. While in Part I of Exhibit 7–7 the work in process and finished goods are included, this has been adjusted in Parts II and III by using much lower turns for the "A" and "B" areas than are possible. Work in process will be discussed in greater detail later in this chapter.

Exhibit 7-7 Normal Inventory versus ABC Inventory

	Monthly Average Requirement	Average Inventory (Months)	Investment
I. Normal Method (All items treated in a similar manner)	$1,000,000	3.5^1	$3,325,000
II. ABC Method			
"A" Parts (5% of items, 75% of cost, 5% of shortages)	$ 750,000	1	$ 750,000
"B" Parts (20% of items, 20% of cost, 20% of shortages)	$ 200,000	2	$ 400,000
"C" parts (75% of items, 5% of cost, 75% of shortages)	$ 50,000	3	$ 150,000
			$1,300,000
		Average Reserves (30%)	390,000
		Possible Obsolescence (2%)	33,800
		Average Turn (6.96)	1,723,800
III. Savings			
Total investment released to cash			$1,601,200
% of inventory released to cash			48.16%
Cost of money savings (at 12%)			$ 192,144
Obsolescent savings (5% versus 2%)			$ 141,200

^{1}Includes 5% obsolescence $175,000; represents a 3.32 times turn annually.

For items in the "A" group, constituting 5 percent of the parts, 75 percent of the cost, and 5 percent of the shortages, the monthly requirement is $750,000 (75 percent of $1,000,000). The average inventory required is one month's supply, so the average investment is $750,000.

For items in the "B" group, constituting 20 percent of the parts, 20 percent of the cost, and 20 percent of the shortages, the monthly requirement is $200,000 (20 percent of $1,000,000). The average inventory required is two months' supply. The average investment is thus $400,000.

For items in the "C" group, constituting 75 percent of the total parts, 5 percent of the cost, and 75 percent of the shortages, the monthly requirement is $50,000 (5 percent of $1,000,000). The average inventory required is three months' supply; thus the average investment is $150,000. With an average reserve of 30 percent, or $390,000, and possible obsolescence of 2 percent, or $33,800, the average investment totals $1,723,800, providing an average turn of 6.96.

Instead of an average investment of $3,325,000, as would be required under the normal method, the ABC method, by requiring only $1,723,800, avoided the expenditure of 48.16 percent of inventory, or $1,601,200 in cash. The cost of savings on money, figured at 12 percent, is $192,144. By reducing the obsolescence factor from 5 percent to 2 percent, there is a further savings of $141,200. This reduction in obsolescence is possible because the high-investment items are watched more closely, and turning them more frequently eliminates, or at least greatly reduces, their numbers at a point where they might become obsolete, especially if an engineering change committee program is functioning effectively, as discussed in Chapter 8. It should be noted that, for purposes of simplicity, work in process (WIP) and finished goods have been ignored in this example.

Exhibit 7–7 conclusively illustrates that even in a small operation such as the one described, great savings can be realized through the implementation of an ABC inventory control program. The direct relationship between "A," "B," and "C" parts and potential shortages, as well as the inverse relationship to cost, provides a convincing argument that the small effort required to institute such a control program is extremely worthwhile.

Some of the many advantages of ABC that are not apparent on the surface are that it:

- Allows lowest possible inventory investment.

- Permits fewest shortages.

- Minimizes placing salespeople in the position of having promised orders delivered late, or at least seriously late, due to waiting the full lead time for the replacement of stocked-out parts.

- Allows lowest percentage of stockouts.

- Enables quickest possible recovery from shortages.

- Allows lowest cost for purchasing in quantities, including a system that permits blanket orders.

- Allows lowest cost for manufacturing parts in quantities and minimizes teardowns and setups.

- Results in faster and better customer service.

- Allows best reaction to unexpected growth because of the reserves in "B" and "C" parts and the strict control and blanket orders for "A" parts.

- Maximizes the use of direct labor by proper scheduling.

- Minimizes the need for indirect labor and excess handling.

- Permits concentration on purchasing to reduce costs.

- Reduces obsolescence.

- Simplifies record keeping and reduces its cost.

- Forces management's attention toward accurate sales forecasting.

- Permits orderly (and frequently the simplest) shop functioning.

Economic Order and Reserve Quantities

Once the ABC method of inventory control has been established, it is possible to take advantage of a beneficial bonus by determining the economic order quantity (EOQ). The EOQ occurs when the cost of *carrying* any item in inventory equals either: (1) the cost of procurement, or (2) the cost of originating a manufacturing order.

Not to be ignored in calculating the cost of procuring the item from an outside source is the expense of a purchase order. Analysis shows that it can cost between $25 and $50 or more to issue a purchase order and, naturally, this goes up every year. You will have to calculate your own cost by dividing the number of orders issued per year into the cost of the purchasing and receiving departments.

Only after a company determines the paperwork and setup costs of an item can it decide how much of that item it can profitably carry in inventory. Let us say, for example, that a company uses 12,000 of one type of screw per year. This item is so inexpensive that the total cost of carrying it in inventory for an entire year is only $30. At the same time, the company's purchasing department determines that it costs $30 to purchase and receive this item once a year. The company then knows that it should order a year's quantity of this item at a time. If, on the other hand, a company uses 12,000 expensive axles per year, the cost of carrying these items in inventory will obviously be much more than the cost of purchasing and receiving once a year. This kind of "A" or "AA" part should be closely scheduled almost on a daily basis, but purchased on an annual or semiannual (blanket) contract.

EOQs used to be calculated using circular slide rules; today the numbers are simply fed into a computer which calculates the EOQs in a fraction of the time it once took. Fundamentally, all that is needed is the cost of the part, the cost of setup or procurement, and the cost of carrying inventory.

My own rule of thumb always has been that inventory should not be carried for more than a year regardless of the outcome of an EOQ determination. Too many factors can change over a long period of time. The item could become obsolete, a design change could drastically reduce the need for the part, or for any number of reasons the finished product could be eliminated from the company's sales line. This is of course less true for "C" parts than it is for either "A"s or "B"s, yet in the main it is a good guideline to follow. Another advantage of such a rule is that renewing a standard part will provide an opportunity to discuss whether the rule applies properly to that particular part or raw material or whether extenuating circumstances demand special handling.

The EOQ acquires increasing importance in any control program as the cost of materials increases. Under low inflationary conditions, it is customary to figure the cost of carrying an item in inventory for a year at 17 percent of its purchase price, including the liability of obsolescence. But as inflation increases and when prices are erratic, that cost can run closer to 35 to 40 percent, and more on some, depending on out-of-pocket interest costs. At that rate, there is real incentive to reduce inventory costs substantially, particularly on items in the "A" group.

Let us use as an example a situation in which a reserve quantity of 50 units of a particular item has been established. Let us also assume that there is a requirement for 400 units in a three-month period in addition to this reserve of 50 units.

Under conventional practices, a purchase order would be issued for 400 units, since the reserve of parts would be continually maintained. Over the three months the company's inventory would hold the reserve of 50 units, plus an average of 200 units as the 400 units declined (400 ÷ 2). Inventory averages 250 units (200 + 50 reserve). We have estimated that 400 units will be needed for three months, or 133 per month. The first month 450 will be available, the second month 317 (450 − 133), and 184 (317 − 133) at the beginning of the third month. It isn't until the end of the last month, in other words, that the company has much danger of a stockout.

If, however, orders were placed for the 400 units under a calculated economic order quantity program, but were scheduled to be delivered at four regularly spaced intervals of 100 units each during the same three-month period, the cost of carrying inventory would be reduced and the chances of a stockout would be nearly eliminated. Any stockout would be alleviated within one week.

The inventory on the date of receipt would be 100 units, covered by a 50-unit reserve for a 50 percent coverage, whereas the inventory of 400 would be covered by the same 50 reserve, giving only a 20 percent initial coverage. If delivery is taken in 100-unit quantities weekly, the stockout probability would drop from roughly 20 to 25 percent to 2 to 3 percent. In addition, because of the frequency of shipments, the recovery time would be much less, thereby causing less disruption to production and delivery promises. Equally important, shop cycle time would also be improved, as will be discussed shortly.

This chapter has already discussed how reserve quantities are largely a matter of judgment, statistical analysis, and cost evaluation. Let us now expand our discussion of reserve quantities.

First take a look at Exhibit 7–8. Here we see a statistically calculated stockout for a product. You can see that if this were an "A" part, a substantial investment theoretically would be required to achieve a low stockout probability. Achieving the same low stockout level if it were a

Exhibit 7–8 Probability of Stockout at Various Inventory Levels

Inventory Level as a Percent of Forecasts

Demand (%)	Probability of Stockout
100	55.0
105	47.0
110	39.0
115	31.0
120	24.5
125	18.5
130	13.5
135	9.5
140	6.5
145	4.5
150	2.8
153	2.0

"C" part would not require a large investment, but it would be wasteful, especially when coverage can be handled through previously discussed ordering techniques, as demonstrated by the sawtooth graph.

Keep in mind that you want to reduce the shortages (70 to 75 percent of which are in "C" parts) and cut the investment (90 to 95 percent of which is in "A" and "B" parts). Actually, what you're trying to achieve is a stockout rate of 5 to 10 percent which will characteristically give you a fill rate of 98 to 99 percent.

The trick is to handle the two categories ("C," and "A" and "B") entirely differently. On the "C" parts, one large buy a year should be made at the best possible price. Delivery should then be scheduled once (or no more than twice) a year, in line with your EOQ determination. Going back to the sawtooth chart in Exhibit 7–6, you can see that the "C" items will largely cover themselves for most of the year. Only as you get down to the end of the order will the real safety stock be needed. Besides, "C" parts are usually standard parts which can be replaced quickly with very little lead time, so a big safety stock is generally not needed.

"A" parts, on the other hand, theoretically need a large safety stock because they ordinarily have a long lead time and are usually built to order. However, if a year's quantity is negotiated, the purchasing department has a chance to obtain the best possible price because the vendor is assured of the business, can schedule the run or runs to the best economies, and will be able to hold inventory.

In turn, all "A" and "B" items can be purchased according to their EOQ calculation but can be scheduled more frequently if desirable, thereby increasing inventory turns and conversely minimizing investment. While it is true that receiving and handling costs rise slightly, investment and cycle times drop substantially. Equally important is the fact that parts are received more frequently, thereby reducing the chance of run-out and shortening replacement time to much less than the lead time. This is an extremely important point to remember. The more frequently a part is brought into the plant, the shorter its stockout period will be. The part's safety stock as a percentage of the whole is also much greater. Another benefit is that you are now in a position to cope with a sudden surge of demand.

To demonstrate that this is so, again turn back to Exhibit 7–6. If the part is brought in every 2 1/2 months (250) and your safety stock is 50, you have a 20 percent ($50 \div 250$) safety stock. But Exhibit 7–6 shows that 20 percent doesn't give you much protection. However, at the same level of monthly usage (100), if the part is brought in once a month with the same safety stock (50), your protection is 50 percent ($50 \div 100$). A look at Exhibit 7–6 shows you that you're beginning to achieve a reasonable level of protection. More importantly, if you do run out, you don't have to wait the two months lead time for this product because you know you'll be getting another shipment sometimes within 30 days, and statistically this shouldn't average more than two weeks ($30 \div 2$ days). This minimizes the time you're out of stock, doesn't disrupt either the shop or service to customers for very long, and keeps your fill rate high.

It is vital that economic order reserve quantity be thoroughly understood by the purchasing manager. It is beneficial to spend time to make certain that the purchasing manager sets up such a program, and to supply information on the subject, if necessary. Purchasing staff must understand that this technique is needed to reduce the cost of carrying inventory; cut the liability of obsolescence; trim the cost of purchase orders; and most important, greatly reduce the probability of stockouts. Manufacturing and production control personnel should also understand these tenets.

Shop Cycle Times

This chapter thus far has intentionally ignored work in process (or throughput time) in order to simplify the discussion of the ABC concept. In closing out this chapter, however, let us at least briefly outline this key area.

Try to estimate the percentage of time a typical part is worked on in a typical manufacturing facility. If you guessed 1 percent you are too high. Startling as this figure may be, it is true. Walk your shop and evaluate your in-process inventory. How long does it take a part to get through the plant? Then look at the part's process sheet. How long does it take to perform all the processes? It is a tiny fraction of the time that the part spends in the shop. Now you see why you keep the "A" and "B" parts moving more quickly and in smaller quantities. Remember, they are 90 to 95 percent of your investment.

Long cycles result from large accumulation of in-process items between each operation. Try to eliminate these accumulations with smaller batches and greater flowing of the parts between operations. In Chapter 11, numerically controlled machines will be discussed. One of the great advantages of some of the new machining centers is the combination of a number of operations at one station, thus eliminating many "floor-to-floor" operations, and speeding up the cycle or throughput time, to say nothing of improving customer service. This is an area that can and should contribute dramatically to any cost reduction effort.

8

Product Redesign

One of the greatest opportunities for profit improvement lies in the redesign of existing products. Through proper redesign efforts, not only can material, labor, and factory burden costs be reduced, but the price and quality of a company's products can be improved and become more competitive.

Despite the tremendous value of product redesign, most companies place very little emphasis on this technique, and therefore do a very poor job of it. It is a shame that so many companies fail to redesign their products on a regular basis. What is even more damaging, is that so many companies want nothing to do with redesigning products; they act as if they'd like the problem to disappear. But it won't disappear, because it is perhaps the most effective way that the cost of producing a product can immediately and substantially be reduced. In this fast-moving day and age, product redesign should become a routine procedure. Products must continually be reanalyzed with redesign in mind, and the approach should be objective, regardless of who designed or authorized the original product.

Selection of Product

The need to redesign an existing product can arise from a variety of different circumstances. Sometimes, for example, a product can no longer be sold profitably without a thorough overhauling of its structure and components. Or perhaps a competitor has made important technological or practical advancements, making your product virtually obsolete. Or maybe the cost of the product's raw materials has increased to such an extent that the finished product is no longer profitable. In other situations, a product needs to be redesigned due to changes in the state of the art caused by any number of external factors. In the automobile industry, for example, car manufacturers have had to almost completely redesign their products due to the recent demand for smaller, more fuel-efficient automobiles. They also have redesigned in order to obtain greater use of robotics in the manufacturing process. (See Chapter 11.)

Products that are no longer competitive in the marketplace need to be redesigned, but so do popular products. Why change the winner? Because their volume will permit you to redesign profitably. In many cases, only the inside working parts of a popular product need to be redesigned in order to cut costs, while parts that the buying public sees and which appear in advertisements will not be altered at all. In other instances, the external appearance of a product will be altered, since the public is known to appreciate restyling and modernization.

Regardless of the popularity of a product, existing products should be redesigned on a regular basis in order to cut costs, maintain or improve profit and quality, and keep up with artistic, technological, and state-of-the-art advancements. It is important to remember that our general knowledge is currently doubling every five to ten years, resulting in a decrease in the life cycle of the average product.

In many cases an external situation will arise, such as a competitor's advancement or a sudden dramatic increase in the cost of the product's primary material, which will necessitate a redesign effort.

All things being equal, the best method of selecting products to be redesigned is to use a variation of the ABC method described in the previous chapter. Just as a small percentage of parts make up a large percentage of material costs, you will also find that as little as 1 percent of a company's products provide 40 percent of sales, while perhaps 5 percent of the number of products provide 70 percent of sales. It is this 5 percent designated as "A" products that should be analyzed for redesign on a regular basis.

Just as an ABC stratification system allows a company to align its priorities so that the most expensive items receive the greatest cost reduction attention, so too should a redesign program concentrate on the items that contribute most to the company's bottom line. A redesign program can then be further refined by linking some of the lower sales volume items to each of these "A" products and making families out of them. (The new term for this is "group technology.") In this way, some of the less popular models will be redesigned along the way. Furthermore, with the new manufacturing equipment today, the "family" or "group" concept becomes more important to increased productivity and reduced setup and down time. Standardization of both material and design will also result. Both are important cost reduction techniques on their own and are discussed in detail elsewhere in this text.

Remember that in our ABC inventory control system described in Chapter 7, parts were classified according to unit value, not total value. This is not the case when choosing the products to be redesigned. Your company might sell only a handful of its top quality, top-of-the-line items. Clearly, these products do not have top priority when it comes to redesign.

At the same time, however, it is important to keep in mind that once an "A" product is redesigned, the same process should be conducted for all related items. Let us say, for example, that you are the president of a sporting goods company. You may sell a half-dozen models of a baseball catcher's shin guard, but the medium priced model accounts for, say, 80 percent of your sales. This medium-priced item is obviously an "A" product and will be one of the first items to be redesigned. If, however, a part is standardized or eliminated in this "A" item, chances are that the same change can be made in the five other shin guards. In other words, once a change is made, the entire product family, regardless of the ABC classification of the individual items, should usually be included in the same redesign effort. Put another way, any redesign of a family of products should seek to standardize and simplify as many parts as possible throughout the entire family or group.

Product Redesign Committee

Every manufacturing company should have a redesign committee made up of the purchasing chief, industrial methods or tool engineer, the head of production and inventory control, the top manufacturing executive, and others, to continually review and accept or reject each and every proposed redesign change. In fact, redesign decisions are so important that the product redesign committee should really be chaired by the division president or general manager. No redesign, engineering change, or deviation, no matter how minor, should be put through without the approval of this committee. The only way a company can determine how a particular change will affect profits, pricing, procurement, obsolescence of inventory, and manufacturing capabilities is to involve all the appropriate departmental personnel in every redesign decision. To do otherwise would be to create or perpetuate unnecessary costs by increasing obsolescence, not taking into account the use of existing inventory, and forcing changes that unnecessarily cause shortages and disruptions of production schedules.

One of the most important tasks of a product redesign committee is to decide *when* a change should be made. If the change is made too late, the savings to be realized by the change will be lost or delayed. But if the change is made too early, costly delays and obsolete inventory will result. If, for example, the product design committee determines that a change is to be made on a particular product, they may be able to delay the change at least until the existing inventory of the particular part is depleted.

There is an exception to this procedure. If the redesign is being made because of safety or some other urgent reason, you won't care how much inventory is made obsolete. The redesign should be made immediately. This is not usually the case, however.

During World War II, American industry manufactured a variety of war material as quickly as possible. One of the lessons learned was that most product improvements are not urgent and can be collected until a model change can be implemented. In the production of military airplanes, for example, improvements were being made almost daily, but the pilots needed planes to fly immediately. If the industry had waited to produce the perfect plane, the war would have ended before the first plane had left the plant. Instead, improvements were collected and made over a period of time. For example, a delivery schedule might be established for a series of P47 airplanes. The first series of changes would be made on P47A planes, another for P47B, another for P47C, and so on. In the production of any item there comes a point of no return when it is too late to make changes effectively.

It is astounding how many companies have no committee to review and approve redesign proposals. At some companies, engineers put through changes in parts and products at will, without any serious discussion concerning whether the change is actually necessary. One of the most counterproductive and insidious problems industry faces is its failure to control engineering changes or deviations. Such uncontrolled changes lead to inventory obsolescence, surplus scrap, short runs, disrupted production schedules, unfavorable variances, higher costs, and poor customer delivery.

A list of redesign procedures is provided in Appendix II.

"Not Invented Here" Syndrome

One of the biggest problems in product redesign lies in overcoming pride of authorship, sometimes called the "not invented here" (NIH) syndrome. Just as it is difficult for parents to look objectively at their offspring, it is equally difficult for an engineering department to look objectively at one of its own products.

Not only is it difficult for engineers to determine how their own products can be improved, for some reason it is equally difficult for an engineering department to *only* reduce costs. They frequently insist on making a "quantum leap" improvement simultaneously with redesign cost improvements. Redesign changes can be made in order to improve a product, or to reduce costs. They are distinct and separate functions, however, even if in the end one type of redesign often helps the other. The Japanese, for example have learned to copy someone else's procedures successfully before trying to make improvements. We in the United States do not seem to have learned this elementary, but very important lesson.

There are several possible ways to avert the NIH syndrome. They all are intended to give the redesign responsibility to someone other than the engineer who designed the original product.

1. Hire an outside firm to take charge of all redesign efforts. If this option is chosen, be certain to review carefully the capabilities of the person assigned to product redesign and be absolutely specific in the instructions for cost reduction, quality, and performance. (Once when I was a group officer I had a division that manufactured gasoline pumps. At the time the industry was moving away from taller pumps toward shorter ones. A redesign of two models left us without any profit. Our engineer felt he had done all he could to reduce costs. An outside firm was brought in and took $16 out of one pump and $18 out of the other. The monthly savings ran to many thousands of dollars.)

2. Find the maverick engineer in your own organization who doesn't run with the pack. Provide a separate office and a specific assignment, and turn this engineer loose. This approach can be very

successful in certain circumstances. It is a good approach in order to achieve maximum standardization, for example.

3. In some cases you will find total objectivity in your organization. This is unusual, but conceivable if you have the right kind of people. Even in this instance, however, do not allow the same engineers who originally worked on the selected product to have primary responsibility for its redesign.

Regardless of which option is chosen, a complete in-depth analysis should be made of your major competitive products. While the goal should be a 30 percent reduction in costs, the quality and performance of the existing product must not be sacrificed. In addition, prototypes should always be carefully tested.

You may be surprised at the results of a proper product redesign effort. Savings will be obtained, and at the same time quality and performance will often be improved. An initial redesign of a product will often provide ideas for a second redesign of the same product at a later date. And finally, company morale and esteem quite frequently will be improved. Employees will be proud that their company's products are continually being upgraded, and sales personnel will be given a new incentive and a talking point with customers.

Value Analysis

Whereas in negotiations with suppliers a predetermined product is being purchased, value analysis refers to the possible substitution of one item for another. In no way does it matter whether the physical characteristics of an item remain identical, as long as the item performs the necessary function with equal or improved efficiency.

The classic, textbook example of value analysis is a large hotel chain whose supply of nine-ounce water glasses has gradually been depleted and needs replacing. The hotel may not have bought water glasses for a decade or more, and when it contacts its supplier it finds that nine-ounce glasses are no longer a stock item. The hotel can buy the glasses if it insists, but they will be inordinately expensive.

Another supplier, however, manufactures a ten-ounce glass that is substantially less expensive because they carry it as a stock item. The ten-ounce glass serves exactly the same purpose as did the nine-ounce glass. Therefore, through a very simple value analysis process the hotel chain determines it should buy the larger, equally efficient water glass.

Value analysis is often much more complicated, of course. To take the same example, other hotels have replaced their water glasses with ones made of plastic. Before such a decision is made, a variety of factors must be taken into account, including the initial cost of both the glass and plastic items; the cost of breakage, sterilization, and packaging; and consumer preference.

Like the other techniques discussed earlier, value analysis cannot possibly be completed successfully without input from the purchasing department, the department most aware of the various cost-reducing options.

Exhibits 8–1 and 8–2 represent two specific, albeit simplified, applications of value analysis principles. Value analysis involves an organized system of techniques and practices that should be an integral part of every purchaser's (and engineer's) daily actions. A training program in value analysis is often appropriate.

Exhibit 8–1 Value Analysis Example 1

A company manufactures fire-fighting equipment, including a small wall-mounted fire extinguisher. The bracket that is used to affix this model on a wall was for many years made of metal. This bracket has been reduced in size and is now made of plastic, at a savings to the company of 50 percent of the cost of the original bracket.

Exhibit 8–2 Value Analysis Example 2

There are many cases where one particular operation has undergone an entire series of changes over the years through value analysis.

(Continued)

In the 1950s, the exterior moldings on automobiles were attached to the body of the car by a variety of metal clips. The clips were heavy, and attaching them required drilling into the side of a car, locating the clip, fastening it to the fender, and then finally attaching the molding to the clip. The process was time-consuming and costly.

The first improvement that was made was to standardize all the clips. Soon every automobile used the same clip, a step that saved a considerable amount of money.

A few years later, with the advent of plastics, the clips became much lighter and less expensive to produce. The next step, sometime in the early sixties, was to eliminate the fastener altogether by applying the moldings with a double adhesive strip. This did away with the labor involved in drilling the holes and aligning and applying the clamp, as well as obtaining the cheaper cost of strips of adhesive versus plastic clamps. The latest innovation has been to substitute the adhesive strip with an even less expensive new epoxy, which is also easier to apply.

The metal strips on a thirty-year-old car look the same as they do on a brand new car. The difference between how they are fastened cannot be determined by the naked eye, but there is a large internal difference, and a major difference in cost.

Make-or-Buy Decisions

Any consideration of cost reduction involves a tough but elementary decision: to make or to buy. Is it less expensive to manufacture a part than it is to buy it? This should be yet another primary assignment for the purchasing department.

Exhibit 8–3 Make-or-Buy Example

A sporting goods company manufactures top-of-the-line baseball gloves. Like any quality item, the gloves are quite expensive. They're made of quality leather and they're handsewn in the United States. They cost between $100 and $175.

While top-quality gloves are important for this company's prestige, as well as for its overall sales picture, most consumers simply can't afford them. In order to satisfy this much larger market, a less expensive glove is also offered.

An engineer collects data from a number of sources, including such information from the purchasing department as the cost of raw materials, transportation, and labor. It may be determined that the minimum cost of producing an inexpensive glove is $30. Marketing, on the other hand, announces that in order to be competitive and to attract the targeted consumer, the glove has to sell for $19.50.

The next step is for the purchasing department to request bids from outside manufacturers, quite frequently from places around the globe where the cost of living is not as high as it is in the United States. If the purchasing department can find such a line of gloves for $12, obviously the decision will be to buy rather than to make. The company should also take this opportunity to make an in-depth analysis of each component of the $30 cost in order to determine why their in-house costs are so high.

In any comparison of a make-or-buy decision, total costs must be looked at, as well as each individual cost. For example, if a machine part is purchased from an outside source for $10, the total outlay of the company is $10 in direct exchange for a given part. If, on the other hand, the company decides to make the part itself, then they are concerned with the elements that make up the direct costs of producing that part. Direct costs in this case refer to the material, labor, variable, and semivariable costs that directly relate to the part.

Once we know that the part in question can be purchased for $10, this cost must be compared to the cost of manufacturing it in-house.

Material	$3.00
Direct labor	.80
Applicable nonfixed burden	1.60
Total	$5.40

Obviously, the savings here are substantial, but these figures assume a semivariable (nonfixed) burden. If we calculated the cost using full burden, including fixed, it might look like this:

Material	$3.00
Labor	.80
Burden	2.40
Total	$6.20

The saving is still $3.80 using full burden, so it passes the first "make" test. In other words, the numbers make it attractive to make this part in-house. Be aware, however, we have assumed that factory space, machinery, and knowledge all currently exist to make such a part. If this part requires the addition of any capital or heavy expense item, then the calculation must be carried further to determine real payback.

The decision whether to make or buy is, of course, not a difficult one when the cost differential is substantial. If, for example, the in-house price is costed out at $6.20 and the outside price is $10, simple arithmetic demonstrates that it is advantageous to make the part rather than to buy it.

On the other hand, a kind of twilight zone occurs when the cost straddles the outside purchase price. Using our $10 part as an example, suppose that the cost using material, labor, and nonfixed burden came to $9, but the cost using full burden was $10.50. In this case let's say the nonfixed burden was $3.00 and total burden was $4.50.

Obviously, the decision confronting the company would be whether or not to bring the part in-house. If the machinery and space were available and work load was below normal, serious consideration should be given to bringing it in. The reason is straightforward. Of the $4.50 burden, you will absorb $4.00, or all of the nonfixed ($3.00) and two-thirds of the fixed ($1.00). Your inventory investment technically should not increase if properly controlled, and your own workers would be kept busy.

My own view is that all things being equal, I would prefer my company to make a product rather than buy it, if the existing knowledge, equipment, and space are sufficiently adequate. Much of the reason for this belief stems from my feeling that once a product is moved into our plant, costs can be reduced using the cost reduction techniques discussed in this text. Without this kind of confidence, however, it may *not* be wise to bring a product in-house when the cost analysis has proven to be ambiguous. In other words, it is a judgment call. Remember, however, for every product you take out of a plant, you increase the burden for all your other products, and you may be decreasing or even eliminating their profitability as well.

All too many companies ignore the purchasing department when it comes to make-or-buy decisions. Purchasing can make a very vital contribution by asking the current vendor to identify his breakdown of material and labor costs, as well as by ascertaining the lowest possible outside price. Only then will it be possible to compare in-house costs to that of the outside supplier.

The importance to a company of making the correct make-or-buy decision is yet another reason why it is vital that buyers be trained to ask all the right questions, understand the answers, and recognize how best to utilize the information received. Purchasing agents have the outside contacts needed to compare different costs and to determine how and why an outside company is able to manufacture a particular item at a lower cost than in-house capability allows.

The buyer is also the one executive likely to be the most objective decision maker. For example, in any make-or-buy situation, the natural, understandable inclination of an engineering department will often be to use the design it created. The purchasing agent's bottom line, on the other hand, is the same as the company's—a desire to make a product with the most assurance of reliability, highest degree of performance, and lowest cost.

Product Elimination

At some point, your controller, sales manager, or some other executive may recommend eliminating a product that, at least on the surface, seems to be losing money. Although there certainly are circumstances that require the elimination of a product or even an entire line, a top executive should be extremely wary of such requests. In my experience, four factors have usually not been taken into account when the elimination of a product is requested by a subordinate:

1. It is vital to make absolutely certain that the cost information and assigned burden figures that are being used for any kind of

make-or-buy, product redesign, or product elimination decision are accurate. Often they are misleading; sometimes they are totally unrealistic. Standard costs often have little relationship to actual costs, for example (see Chapter 10). This is especially true in the area of burden assignment. Make certain that all your decisions are based on accurate cost data.

2. In many cases, no one has made an in-depth analysis to determine whether the product can be redesigned in order to substantially lower material, labor, and burden costs.

3. There is often no suggested replacement, at least not one that is readily available. This means that the factory burden, selling, and G & A costs for the product to be eliminated will have to be spread across the remaining product lines. This will reduce and may even eliminate the profitability of these remaining products.

4. Often there is no plan for the orderly elimination of the product or product line to keep obsolescence and inventory down to a minimum; the same is true for equipment or plant involved.

Product Addition

There will also be times when it is advisable to add new products, and even to enter entirely new business areas. This is particularly appropriate for companies in mature industries which can identify new ventures that have better growth opportunity. Ideally, any new area should complement existing expertise.

Exhibit 8–4 New Business Example

An $8 million company manufactures elevated work platforms (articulating boom and water tanks) for the fire protection industry. It is a mature market, and the opportunities for growth are slim.

Company management recognizes that they must diversify in order to survive. A marketing study determines that elevating work platforms, used in the construction industry and in industrial plants for plant maintenance, are poised to become a growth industry. Of equal importance is the fact that the product has many similarities to the products already manufactured by the company. A certain in-house expertise already exists, especially in hydraulic design.

This company follows a similar pattern in designing and manufacturing each new product within this new field. For example, for one particular machine there are three major U.S. competitors. The company promptly rents all three machines. Within thirty days, the engineering, marketing and service departments have analyzed the three machines and prepared a detailed report.

There are a variety of shortcomings, including a faulty braking system which could allow a runaway condition when on a slope or grade. This is not a very attractive characteristic for a unit that carries a worker thirty feet in the air. To counteract this problem, two manufacturers have installed springset, electric release brakes. This solves the braking problem, but causes abrupt stops. This too is not very comforting to the person perched thirty feet high.

The division's own product design solves the braking problem by installing a double braking system, consisting of an automatic spring applied brake, actuated only when the operator removes his foot from a foot-operated safety switch in the platform, plus a hydraulic-applied foot brake in the platform, similar to the foot brake on a car.

A variety of other improvements are designed, including the installation of a 48-volt battery system which, compared to the competitors' 36-volt system, adds 33 percent more energy to the battery pack and roughly the same increase to the operating cycle time. A direct-drive connection between the turntable and the chassis is replaced by a rotation system, which provides positive but smooth rotation and prevents any possible movement from an external force. Still another improvement is the use of a chrome plated pivot pin with teflon bushings. This eliminates the need for lubrication, which, according to the study conducted by the division's service department, customers frequently overlooked anyway. A rheostat control provides an inexpensive but effective variation of speeds to all function movements. And finally, the prototype is outfitted with 33 feet of working height, two feet higher than its tallest competitor. As an overall goal, an attractive design is stressed.

(Continued)

The marketing department is convinced that it has developed a better machine than what is presently on the market, but also knows that it is going to cost more to build. One suggestion is to take a smaller margin, but that is immediately rejected. There is no point building the machine if it can't be sold profitably. The list price of the newly designed product is subsequently placed $2,000 higher than the price of its nearest competitor.

Two prototypes are built. The first is given to the division's engineering department for testing purposes.. It is sent into the field for evaluation. Improvements are made, and various components are tried in order to determine which ones work best. The second prototype is painted and given to the sales department so a marketing effort can be initiated. Sales literature, publication advertisements, direct mailers, and sales videos are all prepared, and the unit is taken to trade shows. The comments from vendors and potential customers are then applied to the final design.

On the surface, the odds might seem to be stacked against this company. This company is quite late in entering the very competitive elevating work platforms business. In fact, there are already 8 U.S., 4 Japanese, 2 German, 2 French, 2 English, 1 Finnish, 1 New Zealand, and 1 Australian manufacturers of competitive boom products. Even more disturbing is that the company's product is more expensive than any of its competitors.

This company has an ace in the hole, however. It may sell the most expensive product, but it also is confident that its product is worth the higher cost; that important improvements have been made and it is therefore the best quality machine available.

In ten years this company grows 500 percent and increases its profit margins by significantly more than that. Today it is number two in the industry, with a 24 percent share of the U.S. market. It is poised to enter the international marketplace with a product that has a proven track record.

Summary

The savings that can be realized through a comprehensive and proper redesign effort fluctuate widely depending on the extent of the redesign. The standardization of three different screws into one will obviously effect a smaller savings than the redesign of a complicated control valve that reduces both the number of moving parts and the size of the valve's body. Both are important changes, however. Be assured that product redesign can save substantial sums of money and therefore can have a dramatic effect on profit (assuming the savings are not given away unintentionally, as will be discussed in Chapter 10). Conscientious redesign should be able to reduce your costs by a range of 10 to 50 percent. The bulk of the savings will be achieved in the labor, material, and burden areas.

I am so convinced of the benefits of product redesign that I have a standing offer to our division presidents that the corporate office will pay for any product redesigned for cost reduction purposes that does not result in a 10 percent savings. The only proviso is that the corporate office must choose or agree with the division's choice of the firm or personnel in charge of the redesign effort. So far we have never had to pay the cost of a division's redesign effort.

Product redesign should be an area of continuing management attention. A multiyear schedule or Gantt chart should be established, based on an "A"-category and family-group priority system. (A Gantt chart, named after Henry L. Gantt, is a scheduling chart used by industrial engineers and construction people.)

Chapter 11 will discuss the recent revolution in numerically controlled machinery and robotics. Their greatest effectiveness results from standardization of related parts and families of parts (also called group technology). Techniques that only recently have been made available must of course be part of any redesign effort.

9

Accurate Sales Forecasting

The importance of sales forecasting would seem to be self-evident. A company should have at least a fairly accurate idea of how many units of its product can be sold. If too many units are manufactured, inventory investment and carrying costs increase, as does obsolescence since obsolescence is directly related to inventory investment. If too few products are manufactured, sales are forfeited, customers alienated, and sales personnel frustrated. Nevertheless, in the vast majority of manufacturing operations, sales forecasting is little more than guesswork.

Especially during major changes in the economy or business cycle, raw material and retail demands can fluctuate widely from one period to the next. A sudden change in the economy or in a particular market can almost instantly increase the lead time of a product from three weeks to three or six months. This is particularly true in foundries and forge shops when the business cycle has a sudden upturn after a severe recessionary period. Such sudden, dramatic changes can play havoc with even the best inventory control system. The basic foundation necessary to avoid or mitigate shortages on the one hand and stock overruns on the other is thorough, comprehensive, and accurate sales forecasting based on precise, relevant data. In the absence of reasonably accurate sales forecasts, a company can never be certain of the number of units it should produce. Maintaining effective inventory control therefore becomes difficult, if not impossible.

Furthermore, when a company fails to deliver on schedule, the reason, unless there has been a strike, is usually that production has been hampered by inventory shortages or stockouts which, it may further be assumed, were at least partly due to inaccurate sales forecasts. Faulty sales forecasting is a needless common weakness in a great many manufacturing operations, and it is a costly extravagance. Yet reliable sales forecasting is achievable within limits and is comparatively inexpensive.

In the typical American manufacturing operation, however, no one bothers with most of the pertinent figures, such as the forecasts and trends for the particular industry in question, the company's past seasonal or cyclical fluctuation patterns, overall economic indices, and the company's own historical data. (See "Four Basic Elements of Sales Forecasting" later in this chapter.)

Overreliance on Salespeople as Forecasters

Much of the inaccuracy of sales forecasting is a result of relying too much on the opinions of salespeople in the field. This is a fundamental error made by a great many sales managers, and in turn by many presidents and chief executives. While the projections by salespeople in the field are necessary in the preparation of sales projections, they should be only one ingredient in a comprehensive study.

It is unfair to salespeople to expect them to supply the figures on which production schedules will be based. After all, this is not their job. Although individual salespersons, or at least the head of the sales department, should be expected to have some input, they should not be cast in a responsible role in scheduling production, nor should their estimates be translated literally or in raw form into production planning. Besides, by nature and by training, sales personnel are optimists and hate to sell from empty shelves. They would rather have full shelves than empty ones no matter how quickly or slowly they are able to move their products.

In addition to estimates by sales personnel, a sales forecast should include input from several sources. It should include figures showing the forecasts for the industry in which the company operates; forecasts for the economy as a whole; and correlative indices, selected because traditionally or historically they parallel or otherwise have some relationship to the company's own markets. These figures, weighed by their significance and estimated accuracy, must then be measured against the historic trend line of the sales of the company's key products or product lines.

By carefully assessing all of these pertinent factors, it should be possible to adjust estimated sales figures for each key model or product to within 10 percent of actual sales. It should be noted that sales "forecasting" is actually a misnomer, since no prediction can be expected to be 100 percent accurate.

One suggested example of the kind of procedure that should be followed is to have salespeople comment on the trend lines for their product areas. As a management consultant responsible for setting up clients' inventory and production control systems, I used to begin with historical product data complete with trend lines adjusted for seasonal changes. These lines then would be extended to the coming year.

I would then ask the sales personnel to comment on these trends. This estimate based on personal experience was always an invaluable addition to established data. The sales personnel might tell me, for instance, that one particular product would follow the trend line closely, that another would sell an extra 10 percent because the sales force was featuring it, and that yet another would be down 20 percent from the trend line projections because it was gradually being replaced by a newer model.

As a further complication, there are certain items that inexplicably disappear from the retail shelves no matter how many are manufactured or shipped. Production may continually have to be increased on these items, no matter what the trend line or sales forecast projections predict. This is yet another example of buying the suit of clothes and tailoring it to fit your needs.

In Chapter 7 it was explained that by dividing parts into three distinct categories, a manufacturing operation is able to focus on the items that make up the largest percentage of total material costs. A similar distribution often exists in sales. In a typical company, for example, 1 percent of products may contribute 40 percent of sales, 5 percent may contribute 70 percent of sales, and possibly 12 percent will contribute 80 to 85 percent of sales. These numbers will of course vary from company to company, but the premise is sound: a small percentage of a company's products will usually make up a large percentage of sales.

Case Study

Exhibit 9–1 depicts an actual case study of a company that has done a poor job of sales forecasting. The sales manager of this company was asked to prepare a three-month sales forecast for each of the products that constitute the company's most important line. The quarter-year actual sales have been compared with the sales manager's forecasts.

Note that the sales manager predicted that his department would sell 275 units. In reality, 359 units were sold—30 percent over the estimate. It is obvious that there were painful and costly delays in delivery when orders arrived for more units than the production department had planned to produce. In most companies, such unexpected pressure for production would result in a crippling stockout of the bulk of its parts inventories.

Not only was the sales manager far off the mark in projecting total sales, he missed by wide margins in estimating the sales of individual models. This is particularly damaging. Even when the sales manager was accurate in his forecasts, as with model 22R where the sale of 45 units was projected and 45 were actually sold, there were two months out of the three, February and April, when there were serious problems. The figures show clearly that the company must have experienced great difficulty in meeting its delivery schedules.

Exhibit 9–1 Comparison of Typical Sales Forecast with Actual Sales

Model	Monthly Forecasts	Feb.	Actual Sales Mar.	Apr.	3-Month Ave.	Sales as a % of Forecast
20–1	20	31	26	33	30	150
20–3	40	28	33	66	42	105
20–4	15	6	24	13	14	93
22	15	26	48	37	37	247
22R	45	53	29	50	45	100
50	20	43	27	47	39	195
23–23D	5	5	10	3	6	120
120–122						
–S.B.	15	11	55	(2)	21	140
226–506						
–236	50	39	88	73	67	134
600–700	50	36	79	58	58	116
Total	275				359	130

Making an educated guess is one thing. Simply guessing is something else. In this instance the sales manager solicited the opinions of the sales force, then added his own thoughts. Possibly he even made a survey of some kind, on his own. He did not, however:

- Check forecasts for his industry.

- Try to learn what competitors were planning.

- Study the forecasts for the total economy.

- Examine the phase of the current business cycle and the expected phases for the forecasted period.

- Consult trends and projections in correlative indices.

- Work from a historic trend line that had been established from his own sales records.

- Give consideration to seasonal patterns and adjustments.

- Develop individualized pressure curves.

As a result, he not only missed the total forecast by a painful margin, he also failed to forecast the sales of eight of the ten models.

No reasonable production schedule could be maintained on the basis of this report. Estimates were off by 50 percent on the first model; 5 percent on the second; 7 percent on the third; 147 percent on the fourth; 95 percent on the sixth; 20 percent on the seventh; 40 percent on the eighth; 34 percent on the ninth; and 16 percent on the tenth. On average, he missed by 30 percent.

No one should expect sales forecasting to be totally accurate right down to the last model unit, or even always to be accurate to within 10 percent of actual sales. But estimates can and should be made on the basis of reliable research, rather than on instinct or guesswork as is most often the case. In addition, to the extent that parts are standardized, added flexibility can be obtained by switching parts between models in order to alleviate shortages.

Possibly the most common, and most serious, omission in sales forecasting is a failure to consider the influence of seasonal factors on sales. By studying monthly sales over a multiyear period, a trend line can be diagrammed, from which an estimate of sales can be projected.

**Exhibit 9–2 Trend Line of Seasonal Indices Compared with
Undisciplined Forecasts**

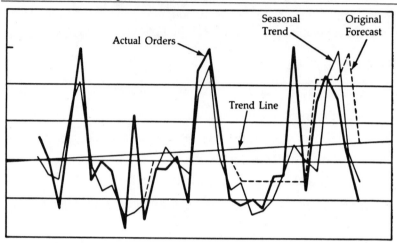

J F M A M J J A S O N D	J F M A M J J A S O N D	J F M A M J J A S O N D
Two Years Previous	Last Year	Present Year

Seasonal Trends ————
Actual Orders ████
Original Forecasts – – – – – –

Study the graph depicted in Exhibit 9–2, which compares a typical company's actual sales for the previous two years and the present year with projections. Note that there is a rising multiyear trend line which must be calculated into future sales estimates. In this instance, the head of sales gave a good forecast, adjusted seasonally. The calculated seasonal trend was quite accurate for all three years and better than the raw forecast.

Historic Trend Lines

Creating a chart showing a historic trend line with seasonal fluctuations should be one of the first priorities in bringing a degree of accuracy to the vital assignment of estimating future sales. Such a chart should then be combined with other historical information. The state of the economy, for example, has a profound effect on sales of any kind. A projection of sales must be made against the background of the overall state of the economy, as measured by the major economic indicators. If there is a drop in the trend line for the gross national product (GNP), for instance, the person charged with forecasting a company's sales should check back to see what happened to sales the previous times the GNP slowed by the same rate. Such statistics as the unemployment rate, retail sales, and unsold inventories should also be considered.

These data are appropriate for general comparisons. In addition, comparisons should be made with correlative economic indicators that have demonstrated their direct bearing on or visible relationship to the sales of the particular company. In some cases, the appropriate data will be obvious. A manufacturer of component parts for kitchen appliances, for example, certainly would want to measure the figures for building construction, housing starts, real estate sales, and the home mortgage market. Other appropriate data might not seem so obvious. It may be that the same indicators used for a company manufacturing kitchen component parts are also essential in forecasting sales for lawn mowers or laundry detergents. New car sales are used by many department store retailers in forecasting their own sales in dry goods, softwear, and hardware.

It is vitally important to determine the most reliable economic indicators that, though perhaps seemingly unrelated, presage or foretell trends in sales in your own industry. It is often a good idea to ask for professional help from the economics department of a local university in setting up your own correlative studies. Once established, they can be maintained in your own shop, or a university-based economist can supply the quarterly figures of your company's particular correlative indices. Whenever possible, historic trend lines should be developed for each product or product group. In other words, the lowest forecastable denominator is desirable.

Used properly, all of the economic indicators that go into sales forecasting can help with other decisions as well, such as when it is prudent to intensify or cut back on advertising; when it is wise to extend credit to customers; even when expansion is justified.

Four Basic Elements of Sales Forecasting

In any sales forecasting analysis, there are four basic elements of economic data that should be used:

- Trends
- Cycles

- Seasonal variations
- Irregular variations

It is necessary to understand each of these terms. Even if you do not maintain your own indicators, as a top executive you must know enough to ask the appropriate questions of internal or consulting experts, and to understand the information furnished you.

Trends are the long-term, long-range movements of a series of economic data. They have little relationship to the month-to-month changes that take place, and they manifest their direction slowly.

Cycles are of shorter duration, though generally unspecified in length, and they are usually featured by alternate periods of expansion and contraction. Their duration may vary widely, as may their intensity in either direction.

Seasonal variations occur within a certain period of the year and recur at about the same time and to approximately the same extent from year to year. Changes in intensity are generally in agreement with the long-term trend line.

Irregular variations are the result of unforeseen or nonrecurring events that have an economic influence. A strike in a key industry, for instance, might cause an irregular variation.

Elements within these four categories may be utilized collectively or separately, and components within them may be used in projecting estimates. One prestigious analytical firm employs what they call *time series analysis* in assisting major retail clients to make their sales forecasts. This is a statistical technique that separates the cyclical and secular (or trend) forces from other types of forces, particularly those due to seasonal factors.

Though such analyses might not apply directly to a manufacturing operation, it is worth noting that they are used in the most sensitive of all sales forecasting, retail sales. Their premise is that the relative importance of the seasonal influence on each month of the year provides an essential guide to retailers in making sound decisions concerning short-term operations. These include determinations of policies in such vital areas as pricing, inventory, purchasing, and size of sales force.

Time series analyses also include such indicators as disposable income, gross national product, expenditures for consumer services, the consumer price index of goods, the consumer price index of services, and expenditures for durable and nondurable goods.

The basics of this approach are applicable to virtually every manufacturing or fabricating operation serving more than one customer. Managers who expect to receive worthwhile sales forecasts from their sales managers should be certain that at least the following has been factored into the analysis:

- The historical trend line of sales in the company, with the seasonal variations clearly identified.

- Forecasts for the industry.

- Forecasts for the nation's economy.

- All available information about the plans of competitors.

- A study showing the status of correlative economic indicators.

In addition, a sales manager's own research should be applied to the analysis. This will include:

- The lines or models that will receive the greatest selling emphasis (advertising, special promotions, discounts, etc.) in the period for which forecasts are being made.

- The lines or models that will be subjected to the stiffest competition from competitors.

- The lines or models that will have the least competition.

- The lines or models being phased out, downgraded, or replaced.

- The "A" item categories comprising the bulk of the sales.

Pressure Curves

One effective way to forecast short-term sales is through the use of pressure curves. A pressure curve, often called a rate-of-change curve, is simply a graph showing the percent change in the twelve-month moving average of any series of monthly numbers. At a glance a company's situation can be compared to its situation at the same time twelve months earlier. This method is sometimes called cycle forecasting. As is true with many of the techniques discussed in this text, you will need an expert versed in this particular procedure to establish and analyze the appropriate series of pressure curves for your company. Even a cursory examination of the pressure curve depicted in Exhibit 9–3, however, will demonstrate the potential value of this technique.

Exhibit 9–3 depicts a twelve-month pressure curve of a $17 million industrial company alongside a graph of that same company's sales volume on a twelve-month moving total basis over a ten-year period. The pressure curve has been calculated by dividing each twelve-month sales total by its level the year before in order to obtain an index figure relative to one hundred. In other words, when the pressure curve is at the one hundred mark it is a signal that sales volume on that twelve-month period is equal to what it was a year earlier.

The pressure curve depicted in Exhibit 9–3 clearly shows that three times during Years 2–10 this company experienced sales at the same level as one year earlier: December of the third year; December of the sixth year; and April of the tenth year. This can be checked by looking at the sales volume graph depicted in Exhibit 9–3 alongside the pressure curve.

More importantly, the pressure curve can be used to predict future sales. Looking at the middle of the ninth year, for example, you will note that the pressure curve is in the midst of a decline. Sales have continued to increase, but at a decreasing rate. This should have served as a warning to this company that it would shortly be experiencing a falling off in sales. In fact, this began to happen about a year later, early in the tenth year.

In order to make effective use of pressure curves, a company should go beyond plotting its own sales volume. Pressure curves can be created from many other internal indicators, including bookings, inventory levels, and operating expenses. In fact, comparing a pressure curve of operating expenses with one based on sales volume will provide a good indicator as to whether the company is decreasing operating expenses to meet an anticipated falling off of sales and, conversely, whether it is appropriately planning to increase expenses when the sales pressure curve is in a recovery and growth mode. Often a company finds that operating expenses have remained stagnant or have increased even in the face of a recessionary dip in sales.

Exhibit 9–3 Sales Volume Pressure Curve

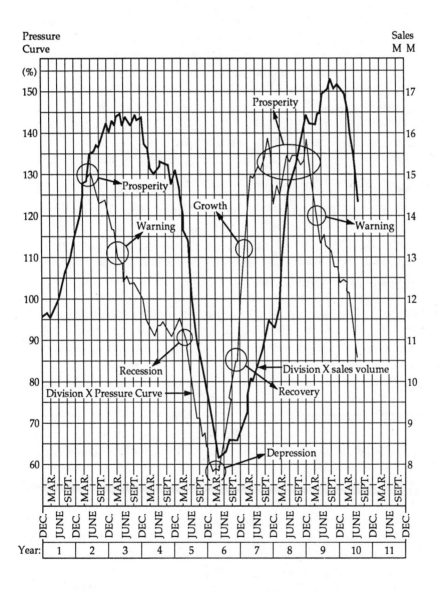

Pressure curves can also be used to plot external indicators that have been found to correlate with your particular company, such as the index of consumer sentiment, housing starts, or automobile or retail sales (see "Historic Trend Lines" section earlier in this chapter). Laid side by side with pressure curves plotting internal data, these pressure curves of external correlative indices will frequently predict the direction and amplitude of the sales volume pressure curve for the short term.

By plotting a company's performance over a number of years and identifying dependable cycles, a pressure curve also allows a company to recognize six phases of each economic cycle. A company can then act accordingly, depending on which phase it is approaching. The six phases are growth, prosperity, warning, recession, depression, and recovery. Note that they are labeled in Exhibit 9–3.

The *growth* phase occurs when conditions are expected to improve. In Exhibit 9–3, for example, this company experienced a growth phase during almost all of Year 8. This is the time when inventories should be maintained at high levels, salespeople should be added, new product lines introduced, advertising and sales promotion increased, and sales training programs accelerated.

The *prosperity* phase occurs when a company is at its pinnacle for that cycle. The gains on the pressure curve become narrower—toward the end of the seventh year and during all of Year 8 in the case of the company depicted in Exhibit 9–3. Although inventories should be maintained at high levels during this phase, a company should begin to plan for darker days. New marketing programs should be begun, expansion programs should be frozen, and, if shortages occur, policies for rationing to customers should be established.

The *warning* phase occurs when business is still increasing but at a decreasing rate. As a rule, this leveling off should occur for three months before this third phase is properly identified, such as during Year 9 in the case of the company depicted in Exhibit 9–3. Once a company enters this phase, inventories should immediately be reduced, advertising should be cut back, and marginal products eliminated.

The *recession* phase occurs when business begins to decrease below the previous year's level—from May of Year 10 according to Exhibit 9–3. During this phase a company should reduce operating expenses as much as possible. It should question the necessity of developing new activities; review and adjust prices; tighten returns from customers; and further reduce advertising, training programs, hiring, and executive travel. It should, however, continue to maintain tight control on quality and customer service.

The *depression* phase occurs when business is still decreasing, but the rate of decrease appears to be bottoming out. Often the losses on the pressure curve will be erratic for twelve months or more. During this phase a company should reduce virtually all advertising; continue its reduction in sales force (although seek to improve quality); continue to reduce and balance inventories; and streamline management, perhaps by combining offices, plants, or divisions. It should also, however, begin to think about the next recovery period. It should begin to plan for long-term growth, prepare sales training programs, and begin to search for top-level people.

The *recovery* phase is probably the most difficult phase to recognize. Business will still be below year-ago levels, but the pressure curve will show that the tailspin has slowed. This is the time to be aggressive so that when the growth period begins you will be ready for it. Work force reductions should be halted, sales training programs reimplemented, new product lines introduced, and advertising and sales promotion reemphasized. In other words, an overall growth strategy should be developed in order to exploit the business upturn that will occur in the near future.

During my nine years in consulting, I always said I could tell which stage of the economic cycle we were in by the type of assignments we received. When a recession was in progress we would get a heavy preponderance of two types of assignments—cost reduction and sales or marketing-related programs (how do we stay profitable and how do we reverse declining sales?).

During recovery stages, on the other hand, we would get a lot of inventory and production control jobs because manufacturing was unable to keep up with sales. I always felt sorry for manufacturing during this stage. Since sales had not forecasted the upturn, purchasing could not get the required parts from the outside because lead time had stretched out quickly and considerably, safety stocks were depleted, and control systems failed.

It's a pretty good rule that when you're certain you're at the bottom of the trough you should make sure "C" part banks are well stocked, "A" and "B" parts are well-covered with blanket orders, and your sources have sufficient stocks on hand to supply you quickly. Load up your safety stocks and keep your key vendors in position to supply increases quickly. Adjust your lead times outwards before they actually hit, thereby triggering your economic order quantity system a little early.

Just to finish my consulting story, assignments were more difficult to come by at the top and the bottom of the business cycle because managements were generally undecided as to which way the economy was going to move so they weren't certain what their needs would be. It is absolutely vital for a company to recognize what stage of the business cycle it is in so that it can act in the appropriate manner. The use of pressure curves is one very effective way to identify each business cycle phase.

End of the Month Syndrome

And finally, there is one other pitfall, called the "End of the Month Syndrome," that can only be avoided by very careful planning. The way this syndrome is allowed to occur, and its painful repercussions, could fill an entire book by itself. Too many manufacturing operations exist in a constant crisis atmosphere. Take, for example, the case of a company with a monthly objective of shipping $10 million worth of its product in order to reach a yearly sales target of $120 million. Ideally, shipments should be spaced throughout the month so that all employees have a steady work load each and every day. But typically, the first week of the month is inordinately slow. Everyone is just recovering from the hectic last week of the previous month, and is happy to take it easy for a few days or to catch up on routine paper work.

Or perhaps a part hasn't arrived on time, or a part has arrived but is defective. An entire manufacturing process may have to be delayed until it is available. In other instances, a customer may have changed his order at the last minute, which will necessitate another kind of delay.

It's the beginning of the month, so no one is too concerned about these minor problems. The pervasive feeling is that there is still plenty of time to meet the $10 million monthly goal. Before you know it, however, it is the middle of the month, and only $1 million worth of goods has been shipped. Suddenly the manufacturing plant is in chaos, with everyone scurrying around in a mad-dash effort to ship $9 million worth of goods in the last ten working days of the month. This inevitably results in poor productivity and wasteful expenditures.

In such a scenario, the purchasing department is placed in a particularly untenable situation. As the end of the month approaches, pressures mount on the purchasing department to obtain needed supplies, regardless of cost, so that the company's monthly quota can be met. This is a sure way to lose control of costs. Quality control will also suffer, as there will be undue pressure to ship everything that comes off the manufacturing floor, ignoring a minor defect that might otherwise have caused it to be rejected. There is also a tendency to reach into the next month and pull out all the "cherries," a decision which will only exacerbate the problem the following month.

Every department contributes to this "End of the Month Syndrome," and every department must be aware of its dangers and plan in advance to avoid it. The marketing department, for example, should not allow customers to frivolously change orders at the last minute. Each department must schedule its tasks so that it is prepared to deliver a consistent performance throughout the duration of each month.

Summary

Armed with all the internal and external data discussed in this chapter, as well as with the estimates of internal sales staff, a sales forecast by model number or product line for the upcoming period, accurate to within 10 percent, should be possible. Only then will a company be able to plan inventory, production control, and schedules successfully. Not only will accurate sales forecasting eliminate costly shortages and surpluses of final products, but, as discussed in the previous chapter, the resulting improvement in your inventory control system will prove to be an additional tool in reducing overall costs in the manufacturing operation.

One piece of equipment which is now in common usage but which was literally unknown when I was starting out is the computer. The amount of data that can be stored and the sophistication and speed of the calculations that can be made by computers today is remarkable. Properly employed in the field of forecasting, computers can provide data for the forecasting of sales that we wouldn't have ever dreamed about just a short thirty years ago. It's too bad they are not better utilized for such purposes.

10

The Pitfalls
of Pricing

The sad irony of the cost reduction program in many companies is that the savings realized after so much hard work and effort can be forfeited by a faulty or misunderstood pricing system. Months and countless hours may be spent restructuring a company's organization, conducting macro- and microanalyses, instituting work sampling techniques and scientific sales forecasting, establishing a proper set of priorities and a standards program, redesigning products, and taking a variety of measures to make certain procurement procedures are operating at maximum efficiency and profitability. But unless top management is aware of the pitfalls of pricing, a company faces the imminent danger of losing part of, all of, or in some cases even more than, its cost reduction savings. You may not even be aware of what has happened until it is too late—until you take a look at the bottom line and can't understand why the substantial savings you realized did not translate into an increase in profit, and why in some cases your profit percentage actually fell.

The Pitfalls of Inflation

Pricing pitfalls are particularly critical during periods of high inflation. In an inflationary economy, there is no cost reduction substitute for pricing. A company can undergo the most comprehensive, most effective cost reduction program possible, but unless the pitfalls of inflation are recognized and acted upon, the savings will be lost, literally within a matter of months, by inflation. Inflation moves so fast and is so far-reaching that it simply cannot be offset by cost reduction alone.

But don't be lulled into a false sense of security by periods of low inflation. To begin with, as will be demonstrated shortly, even without inflation a faulty pricing system can give away all your hard-won cost-reduction savings. In addition, even when the consumer price index is rising by only 5 percent annually or less, the price of certain raw materials vital to your manufacturing operation can suddenly rise much more rapidly. No matter how much your costs increase due to inflation, over the long run it is suicidal not to build those added costs into the price of your product.

The Pitfalls of Stagnation

Whether you like it or not, we have become accustomed to some inflation. What happens if this ceases? Your costs affiliated with personnel will continue to move up. Your electricity, taxes, heat and power will probably do likewise. Now you're squeezed, as you can't pass price increases along to the customer. As a result, you must begin cost improvements in earnest just to maintain past margins, not necessarily to improve them.

The days of protecting customers from price increases for sixty or ninety days should be over. When prices are frozen for three months during a period of 12 percent inflation, about 2.5 percent is suddenly lost forever from the bottom line. At all times, but especially during periods of high inflation, purchasing departments should build and maintain a weighted index of "A" parts and discuss changes weekly with the president. Only then can an intelligent decision be made about when and how much to raise the prices of finished products whose "A" part content is being closely monitored. Remember, increasing prices is the only way to offset the effect of severe inflation.

Over the years, I have found that the best method of determining whether your company's pricing structure is appropriate is to keep a careful eye on the cost of materials as a percentage of sales. As soon as this percentage begins to increase, this is an indication that the company's pricing structure has not kept pace with inflation. This is a very simple and quick indicator, and is virtually foolproof. Some manufacturing and sales personnel may argue that their product mix has changed, but only very rarely will products change so drastically and so rapidly as to justify such an excuse.

The Negative Variance

All too often, standard costs are set with the full knowledge that almost immediately after the start of the new year there will be negative variances in material, labor, or burden (or all three). If you price off standard costs with full knowledge that negative variances will occur early in the year, you cannot attain the budgeted profit unless you make an adjustment to recognize these variances.

It is obviously impossible, however, to run out and alter your pricing every time the cost of an "A" part changes. It is vitally important, therefore, to create a positive variance prior to the beginning of every year. In order to avoid an eroding profit margin, the materials percentage indicator should be adjusted via the weighted "A" part index, which in turn should be revised at the time "A" parts are ordered (certainly no later than when they are received into inventory).

In other words, prices should be raised not only to offset past increases in the cost of materials, but also to offset projected cost increases during the coming year. As soon as sufficient "A" part material price changes are experienced and an approximate level of change can be ascertained, prices can once again be revised in order to maintain a positive variance. There are, however, serious dangers in relying on the standard cost system, as will be discussed in the next section.

The Danger of Standard Costs

There are a number of ways in which a faulty pricing structure can negate the benefits of the savings gained through cost reduction. The most common and most insidious way is if your pricing relies upon standard costs. Standard costs should be called the opiate of managers because it dulls their senses. Rarely do managers understand or appreciate the true effects of standard costs, which are probably the greatest enemy of cost reduction. I recognize that this is an iconoclastic position, but bear with me as I develop the logic behind it.

Controllers and other accounting personnel use standard costs for purposes of pricing inventories and tabulating profit and loss statements. These standards are often used incorrectly to price the items to be sold. When the standard cost of a particular part is estimated, the price used is invariably the price of the item the last time it was purchased by the company. But if the purchasing department has not bought that item for a year or more, this standard price will obviously be too low. In periods of inflation, prices of materials sometimes change monthly, thereby further accentuating pricing errors. If standard costs are too low, the final price of the completed item will also be too low, and profit will soon disappear. In order to begin to correct this problem, the controller should continually update prices from the purchasing department. However, it will never really be corrected if you price off standards.

A parallel problem is that standard prices are often set in late summer or early fall, several months before the calendar year in which they will be used. Even if the purchasing department has given the controller current prices rather than the price from the last time the item was purchased, the standard prices might easily be seven or eight percentage points too low by the time they are actually put into effect. Similarly, the standard price, even if accurate on January 1, will be off base by the end of the year, as inflation takes its toll. In order to achieve any degree of validity, it is vital that standard prices continually be adjusted for inflation, or be set higher at the beginning of the year in order to take into account inflation estimates for the upcoming twelve months.

The price of materials is not the only cost that must be monitored. Negative variances will also occur if a company's accounting department incorrectly estimates other standard costs, such as labor and burden, that are affected by inflation, or any other variable that can be expected to increase prices.

Not withstanding all this, there is one overriding reason why standard costs as used in much of industry today are a serious deterrent to good mangement and reasonable profits. We will call this damaging effect of standard costs "the insidious giveaway," and discuss it in detail in the section that follows.

The Insidious Giveaway

The most frequent and most damaging way in which a faulty pricing mechanism negates the positive results of cost reduction occurs literally every day in this country and has very little to do with inflation. All too often the savings realized through cost reduction are deducted directly off the standard cost of the item, and then a constant markup is used to adjust the sale price, thus reducing or eliminating the benefit of the cost reduction.

Study Exhibit 10–1, which depicts a product that was cost reduced and repriced, only to lose all the savings plus part of the product's original gross profit.

Exhibit 10–1 depicts the cost breakdown of an item for which $5 has gone for materials, $2 for labor, and $6 for overhead. The total cost of producing the item is thus $13, on top of which were added selling and general and administrative costs, plus a 5 percent profit margin, for a selling price of $17.33. The controller has arrived at this final selling price by marking up the standard cost of sales ($13) by 33.3 percent ($13 x 1.33 = $17.33). Selling and general administrative costs are $3.47 (20 percent of $17.33), and pretax profit is $.86 (5 percent of $17.33).

Exhibit 10-1 The Pitfalls of Pricing

	Original Item Cost and Selling Price Using a 33.3% Markup	Subsequent Cost Reduction with the Profit Protected by No Standard Cost Change	Change in Price and Profit When Old Markup (33.3%) is Applied to Revised Cost
Selling price	$17.33	$17.33	$12.00
Material	$ 5	$ 4	$ 4
Labor	$ 2	$ 1	$ 1
Overhead	$ 6	$ 4	$ 4
Total	$13	$ 9	$ 9
Selling and General and Administrative (20%)	$ 3.47	$ 3.47	$ 3.47
Total Cost	$16.47	$12.47	$12.47
Pretax Profit	$ .86 (5%)	$ 4.86 (28%)	−.47 (−2.7%)

Now the controller looks at the new cost figures after a cost reduction program has been implemented. Through the implementation of an ABC inventory classification system and other innovative purchasing techniques, there has been a 20 percent savings in material costs, reducing them from $5 to $4 per item. Ratio analysis, work sampling, redesign, and methods improvement have saved 50 percent of the cost of direct labor, reducing that cost from $2 to $1 per item. And finally, plant consolidation, elimination of some indirect labor, resulting fringe savings, and increased plant utilization based on proper make-or-buy decisions have effected a 33 percent reduction in burden, reducing that cost per item from $6 to $4. Now the total cost of producing this item is $9.00 instead of $13.00—all because of the success of a cost reduction program.

First let's take a look at what happens when the benefits of cost reduction are passed on to the company in the form of profit. Looking at the second column in Exhibit 10–1, we see that selling and general and administrative costs have remained at $3.47. We have done nothing to increase or decrease these cost areas. If we keep the final price of the item at $17.33, our profit has risen to $4.86 ($9 + $3.47 = $12.47; $17.33 − $12.47 = $4.86). Profit as percentage of sales has increased from 5 to 28 percent (28 percent of $17.33 = $4.86). In other words, the hard work that was put into the comprehensive cost reduction program has paid off in the form of increased profits (both dollars and margin), and has made the company more competitive by not being forced to keep raising prices to offset inflation, if it so chooses.

All too often, however, something very strange happens with cost reduction savings that substantially reduces or even eliminates profit. Take a look at the last column in Exhibit 10–1. The controller (or, more likely, one of the clerical personnel), unaware of what has been accomplished through cost reduction, has taken the revised $9 standard costs and applied the same factor for markup (33 percent) that was used in the past. He or she thus comes up with a final selling price of $12 ($9 x 1.33 = $12).

The controller, however, neglected to realize that selling and general and administrative costs have remained at $3.47, and that the effect of a $12 selling price is the total elimination of profit. In fact, the company will lose $.47 on each item it sells, or a swing of $5.33 per item ($4 cost savings x 1.33 = $5.33 price reduction).

Putting it another way, the cost reduction program has eliminated $4 from the cost of the item, but the pricing structure has cut $5.33 from the final price of the item. The controller and possibly the sales manager, by doing what they perceived to be their duty, have taken away more than cost reduction efforts have saved on every unit sold. All the benefits of the cost reduction program and more have gone to the customer, plus the expenses, plus the cost of G & A. Your cost reduction program has been totally neutralized and rendered useless.

This scenario might sound ludicrous. It is. But it occurs, and it occurs both widely and on a daily basis. It probably occurs in your company. Cost reduction will eliminate profit unless the pricing arm of the company recognizes and understands what the rest of the management team is doing. If a constant markup factor is applied to standard costs, and it is revised to reflect cost reduction programs, this scenario will be duplicated. Pricing and standard costs must be completely divorced from one another if cost reductions are to be protected and profits improved.

The controller and the sales manager (or their staffs) are the only people in your organization in a position to give away all that your cost reduction program has gained, in the manner just described. They may think that it is in everyone's best interests to pass along the impressive cost reductions in the form of lower prices. Worse yet, they probably do it mechanically without even realizing it. The result will be the same: to price your company right out of black ink and into the red.

Sales personnel and sales managers will often fight against price rises, arguing that sales will suffer. But if you are selling at a loss there's no point being in business in the first place. What's more, sales personnel are notoriously poor predictors of the effects of a rise in prices. Most of you are familiar with the old saw, "Sure we are losing money on each item, but look at our volume increase!"

A poor pricing policy should by no means be blamed on sales personnel or controllers, however. It is the job of salespeople to sell. They have little way of knowing how much they must charge for an item in order for the company to make a profit. As for controllers, they simply receive notice that the cost of an item is, say $9, mechanically multiply this by a factor of 1.33 to cover administrative costs and profit, and mark the price of the item at $12.00. Controllers usually have no way of knowing that the item sold for much more the previous year, that the cost has been cut due to an intensive cost reduction program, and that by changing the price to $12 the benefits of the company's cost reduction program have actually been negated and the product has been priced to lose money.

It is absolutely vital that after the completion of a successful cost reduction program the savings are not passed along to someone else so that the company actually suffers a loss of income. A company may as well not bother to reduce costs if this is going to be the case. It is remarkable, however, how many companies fail to follow through on pricing and so negate the benefits of cost reduction. In other words, they do not follow through in order to turn their cost reduction into profit improvement. Cost figures are turned over to the controller who is allowed to set final prices in collaboration with the sales manager. Prices are set mechanically off revised standards without regard to protecting or improving profits, and frequently in a perfunctory manner by clerical personnel.

Ultimately, it is the president or chief executive officer who must be responsible for making certain that the controller or another financial executive does not set prices using unyielding formulas that do not take into account the impact of cost reduction. Pricing policy and technique must be administered carefully and policed by the head of the organization, and the key personnel involved must be educated about both proper procedures and the ramifications of improper procedures. Standard costs must be used only for internal purposes, and pricing should become a separate and divorced function based upon other norms. To do otherwise invites disaster.

A Suggested Solution

The preceding pages have demonstrated the dangers of mechanically pricing off standard costs and the importance of creating positive variances. Standard costs should be used only for internal control, not for final pricing. Failure to heed this maxim can, as we have seen, price your company right out of the black and into the red. It is also important to remember that these dangers threaten year after year. If a favorable variance is maintained for twelve months, and then the pitfalls of pricing are once again ignored, the accounting department simply will give away your cost reduction savings in the second year by lowering the standard cost.

This may all seem heretical, but a study of the preceding pages, as well as a little work of your own with a pad and pencil, should convince you that your pricing system must have some kind of built-in protection. Pricing for sales is different than pricing for inventory and shop control.

As a solution, some companies do not report their cost reductions to the controller at all, forcing prices to be set off false standards. Favorable variances can be deferred in inventory and passed to income during inventory evaluation once a year. An inventory adjustment can then be made annually. Other companies simply raise their prices periodically regardless of cost reduction savings, using old unrevised standards adjusted for inflation but not cost reduction. No matter what method you use, someone in your company should be responsible for making certain that cost reduction savings serve to increase rather than decrease profits.

Once the situation is fully recognized and understood, a compromise can often be reached so that some of the savings realized through cost reduction will be passed on to the company in the form of increased profits, and some to the customer through a price reduction if this is deemed wise or acceptable. It depends on the situation.

Returning for a moment to Exhibit 10–1, the controller and sales manager could have taken the $4 that was saved by cost reduction and deducted it from the original selling price of $17.33. This would have resulted in a new selling price of $13.33, a substantial reduction in price that would have provided a good competitive edge, while at the same time permitting the corporation to receive the same amount of money in profit and for selling and G & A expenses as it had the previous year. The amount of pretax profit would have been the same—$.86—but the percentage of profit would have increased from 5 percent (.86 divided by $17.33 = .05) to 6.5 percent (.86 divided by 13.33 = .065). The other measure that should be considered is return on assets, which will vary from company to company.

The solution just described passes all of the cost reduction savings on to the customer. Thirty-one percent ($4 divided by $13) of the original cost of the item was saved through cost reduction, and profit was only increased 1.5 percentage points. It may very well be that this company would want to make more of a compromise between the 5 percent profit depicted in the first column in Exhibit 10–1 and the 28 percent in the second column. Perhaps the company would decide to split the $4 increase in profit ($4.86 – .86 = $4) evenly between profits and the final price, which would mean a $2 increase in profit and $2 reduction in price. The price of the item in this case would be $15.33 and profit would be $2.86. This would serve to increase profit *and* your product's price competitiveness.

There are, of course, an infinite number of ways in which cost reduction savings can be divided between profit and price. The amount of profit a company should take on any one particular item will depend on a variety of factors, most prominent of which are the existing profit percentage, the competition's price for the same item, and the company's desire to increase its share in the marketplace. If, for example, the product was redesigned because it was beginning to lose money, most if not all of the cost savings will have to go to profit. If, on the other hand, the competition is selling virtually the identical item at a substantially lower price, or if the company has decided it is important to increase its share of the market, then most of the cost savings probably should go towards a reduction in the final price of the item, assuming the item is price sensitive.

Regardless of the precise dispensation of the cost reduction savings, what is important is that the company is aware of the entire situation, and makes its decision from a position of knowledge and strength rather than from a position of confusion and ignorance. As with an ABC inventory control system, you have selected a suit of clothes off the rack; now it has to be tailored to your specific needs. And in this instance, it will be a complicated tailoring job indeed.

Case Study

The erosion of profit due to a faulty pricing system occurs literally every day in countless manufacturing companies across the U.S. One company with which I am familiar had an item that cost $10.00 to manufacture and was being sold with a conventional markup of 66.66 percent on the cost of sales, at $16.66 (1.66 x $10 = $16.66).

Cost reduction techniques had cut $1 from the cost—from $10.00 down to $9.00. The controller had passed the figure along to the sales manager, who in turn had priced the model at $15.00—its $9.00 cost multiplied by the 1.66 factor.

The result was that, having saved $1 in production costs, the sales department gave away $1.67 on each model sold. It not only knocked out the dollar that had been saved, it took away an additional 67¢ from profit.

Further investigation revealed that the sales personnel were giving quantity discounts that had absolutely no relationship to the savings that had been realized by the cost reduction program. Sales personnel were taking orders for 10,000 quantities with a standard gross margin of only 13 percent. It was also learned that some of the buyers who placed orders for lots of 10,000 were actually taking delivery of only a few hundred. In addition, groups of individuals were joining together to order in 10,000 lots but requiring deliveries of their portions at diverse locations.

This same company was also found to be marking up its product by 40 percent of its cost rather than to attain a 40 percent gross margin. A 40 percent gross margin requires a 66.6 percent markup (or a multiple of 1.667), while a straight 40 percent markup on cost yields only 28.5 percent of sales (or a multiple of 1.404). For example, if an item costs $6.00 to make, with a 40 percent margin it should sell for $10.00, since 40 percent of $10.00 equals $4.00. A 40 percent straight markup on that same $6.00 item would put its selling price at $8.40, providing a $2.40 gross profit or 28 percent of sales. This probably would not cover the cost of selling and G & A, much less leave any room for profit. The item would most likely sell at a loss.

As emphasized earlier, the fault for any of these errors probably does not lie with sales personnel, most of whom have no idea how much it costs to produce the items they sell. There is no reason why they should since that isn't their job. Rather, the responsibility for maintaining a sensible and effective pricing policy should fall on the top executive, who should keep pricing under continual surveillance. The top executive should also insist that the company's designated financial officer do so as well.

Pricing is the last line of defense both for your cost reduction program and against the ravages of inflation. Establishing prices is the final step after all of the economies espoused in this book have been put in effect. If it is ignored, all that has been gained and more will be dissipated.

Make no mistake about it, pricing is an extremely difficult area to control. There is no foolproof system. The best a company can hope to do is to keep its shop costs and standards totally divorced from pricing. They are two entirely different areas and should be treated as such.

11

Labor Costs and the New Industrial Revolution

The early chapters of this guide demonstrated how labor costs could be reduced quickly through ratio analysis, constant dollar analysis, and work sampling. These techniques, however, were part of a thirty-day "quick and dirty" program and, while effective, in no way pretended to be an in-depth analysis of all the many factors that affect the cost of direct labor.

In subsequent chapters it was explained that despite the natural inclination of many top executives to attack direct labor costs immediately when savings are needed, this strategy was premature. There are several reasons. In the first place, remember that in the average industrial operation direct labor represents only about 10 percent or less of total costs. Material, on the other hand, can represent as much as 40 to 50 percent or more, which is why cost reduction techniques in the purchasing department and other related areas have been emphasized as the higher priorities.

There is yet another, perhaps more important, reason why it is a mistake for a company to attack labor costs early in its cost reduction program. While it is true that substantial savings can be realized through work sampling and constant dollar, ratio, and organizational analysis, the most important method of making certain that labor costs are not out of line is through the implementation of an effective standards program, which can be best performed after at least the superficial fat has been removed from the operation. It is, however, a time-consuming and costly operation.

Labor Standards

The installation of a standards program, that is, a program that defines precisely the length of time and the manpower required for the tasks that must be performed in a manufacturing operation, is no simple procedure. Although when properly maintained it can yield substantial savings, the timing of such a program is extremely important. If standards are installed too early, before unnecessary costs have been eliminated through other, more elementary, cost reduction techniques, considerable time and money will be wasted. Too many managers seem eager to rush in and fine tune an overweight elephant when in fact the entire animal must be trimmed before scientifically engineered standards can be effectively introduced. If, on the other hand, a company attempts to wait until it is running at optimum efficiency, the standards may never be implemented. There is no such thing as a "perfect" manufacturing operation. The timing, in other words, must be a matter of judgment, but in general a standards program should be implemented after a "quick and dirty," thirty-day cost reduction program has been completed and the company has obtained the stability, controls, and trained personnel to undertake a longer-term, more sophisticated program.

Labor standards, also called production standards, is one of the areas of greatest confusion for the average manager. The subject is frequently either misunderstood or ignored. But as a chief executive, you can be assured that if you have no labor control standards at all, your labor costs will be roughly 100 percent excessive. The company will be getting less than four hours of work a day for eight hours of pay. Direct and indirect labor costs, in other words, which together can constitute 15 to 20 percent or more of the sales dollars (with fringes added), will be about twice as high as necessary (as will be demonstrated shortly in Exhibit 11–1). The precise amount of money wasted due to a lack of labor standards will of course vary, depending upon a host of factors. As a rule of thumb, for example, a nonroutine function can be expected to have a lower performance or efficiency level than a routine operation. For example, construction workers are probably less efficient than direct labor in a factory. But regardless of the type of operation, be assured that major savings in the cost of labor can be realized by the implementation of a professional standardization program.

A production standard can be defined as the time required to produce the desired quality product or service:

- By an average, qualified, experienced worker.

- Working at a normal pace.

- Following the standardized method.

- Using the prescribed equipment.

- Operating at standardized feeds and speeds.

- Taking the allowed personal, fatigue, and delay allowances which normally average about 15 percent.

Exhibit 11–1 shows the range of labor excess according to the corresponding type of standard. There are basically three ways in which standards can be determined.

Exhibit 11–1 Spectrum of Labor Cost Excess

TYPE	Labor Cost Excess, %				
	0	25	50	75	100
No Control					
Gross Estimated Standards					
Historical Standards					
Work Sampling					
Engineered Standards—Day Work					
Engineered Standards—Incentive					

Gross estimated standards are simply an educated estimate of how much production will be completed by a machine, function, or operator in a specified period of time. With gross estimated standards, however, excess labor costs can still be expected to average 75 to 90 percent.

Historical standards can be used for an operation that has been conducted in previous years. The company knows approximately what to expect. Historical standards will reduce the excess of labor to 50 to 75 percent.

By far the most effective ongoing standards program is *engineered standards*, which can cut labor excess to 10 percent or less. Notice also in Exhibit 11–1 that work sampling, which was conducted as part of our thirty-day program, ranks quite high in degree of performance.

Engineered Standards

Despite the distinct, proven superiority of engineered standards, it is remarkable how many manufacturing operations in the United States, either through inexperience or lethargy, opt for one of the other two standardization methods, or no method at all. (It is equally remarkable that so many operations ignore work sampling.) Exhibit 11–1 shows that an operation without any controls can suffer up to 100 percent labor excess. Work sampling alone can reduce this to 30 to 50 percent excess, and in some cases even less. Proper engineered standards, on the other hand, can bring excess down to 10 to 15 percent in a day work (nonincentive) system.

An engineered standards program contributes to improved productivity through three specific benefits: methods improvement, time utilization, and a more consistent worker pace. Methods are improved through a better use of station layout, operation motion sequence, proper tooling, and machine feeds and speeds. Time is utilized more productively because its use is being measured and accounted for. In addition, the number of personnel can be reduced. And finally, work pace becomes more consistent because workers know what is expected of them.

Engineered standards can be implemented through the use of either *predetermined time data* or *time study data*. The primary difference is the length of time of the motions (or elements) that are measured. Time study data is concerned with comparatively large segments of time, all of which can be measured by a stopwatch. Predetermined time data measures much shorter periods of time, called micromotions, which are much too short to be measured by a stopwatch.

Predetermined time is by far the more precise, more effective method. The primary problem with a simple time study is that when dealing with the comparatively long elements of time made necessary by stopwatch measurement, a worker can easily beat a company's standard by making minute changes within the long elements of a task. Time studies become loose and inaccurate over a period of relatively few years since changes made within an element can't be restudied, generally because of union contract language.

With a predetermined time standard, the worker's reach or grasp or other minute change is made up of many micromotions. If a manager can show that the worker has changed the micromotions, management can change the standards, since the method has changed and, hence, the standard for the method. This has been well established through arbitration for many years. Predetermined standards can be updated, as is well-established by past arbitration rulings.

Predetermined time data requires the recording and documenting of physical motions and the application of predetermined normal time to each motion. By developing a "library" of work elements and times and selecting those elements that apply to a specific product or task, it is a natural progression to engineered standards.

The introduction of engineered standards involves the highest engineering skills and hence has a high development cost. But once all other cost reduction techniques have been employed, this is the ultimate tool in cost reduction and cost control. It also has one added advantage that many people do not perceive or understand. Armed with the data just described, a company can price a new product before it ever gets to the shop. The company will know what it will cost to build the product, and therefore what price to put on it. Before the first unit is built, its place in the competitive marketplace can, with reasonable accuracy, be determined.

Setting up engineered standards requires the services of qualified industrial engineers trained in this particular field. Methods time measurement and its offshoots have been modified, and there are a number of good reference works dealing with the techniques and modified times. While the installation of a "library" may require the help of a qualified consultant, it can be maintained internally by most any qualified personnel.

Engineered standards are thoroughly acceptable to the unions and should be a part of any well-managed company. It is one of the programs that a good manager should create for long-range, permanent cost reduction.

If you have begun and maintained a work sampling program, you know the results achieved and its cost to maintain. Referring to Exhibit 11–1, you can determine whether the additional improvements to be had from engineered standards are worth additional development and maintenance costs. Do not neglect to include in your calculations an evaluation of advantages in estimating, pricing, methods, and design that go along with a predetermined time system.

Incentive Shops

As can be seen in Exhibit 11–1, the most effective standards are engineered standards in an incentive shop. However, incentive shops have their own unique problems. I am of the school that firmly believes that a 90 percent day work (nonincentive) performance level in the long run will be less expensive than maintaining a comprehensive incentive program. With incentives, in the end there often are little or no cost savings. This is partly due to the fact that incentives only attack the 10 to 15 percent excess that a good day work standards program misses, because any savings over 100 percent performance generally go to the workers.

An incentive program in effect offers workers the incentive to break down the company's standards program. Most importantly, the cost of maintaining an incentive program far exceeds that of a measured day work program and in fact usually exceeds the extra savings the company achieves. Not only do the standards themselves have to be carefully and constantly maintained, but base wages plus incentives must be calculated separately for every employee, for each work assignment, and for each pay period. Obviously, these procedures are neither productive nor cost effective, and add substantially to costs. Other problems with an incentive shop include:

- The workers tend to attack the tightest standards until they are loosened, then move on to the next tightest standard, and so on. The system, in other words, will gradually be loosened or broken.

- The incentive is to break the system and increase wages, not to benefit the company.

- The foreman and quality control inspectors must spend an increasing amount of time supervising.

- Workers will sometimes run a number of pieces before clocking in, artificially inflating both downtime and incentive pay.

- There is an incentive to pass through scrap, hoping to have it counted as good pieces.

- The number of shop grievances tends to increase.

- On machine-paced operations, the operator is paid incentive even when not performing any task.

- The need for time-keepers substantially increases payroll costs.

- Payroll cost calculations skyrocket.

- Workers will tend to hide pieces from an "easy" standard, throwing them into the next run. This creates havoc with count, yield, scrap, inventory levels, and quality records.

New Plants and Equipment

No discussion of reducing labor costs should ignore the often parallel decision as to whether new plant and equipment are needed to increase productivity. This handbook continually has emphasized the value of inexpensive cost reduction techniques. Quite simply, if a company spends a dollar to save a dollar, the effect, at least in the short term, is meaningless. But if that same company spends a dollar to save five dollars, the actual bottom line savings are significant. Virtually all the most important principles discussed previously—from our thirty-day approach, to specific purchasing techniques, to product redesign, to the coordination of a sensible pricing mechanism—are relatively inexpensive to implement. Purchasing new plant and equipment, on the other hand, is by no means an inexpensive venture, and therefore it should not be considered in a cavalier manner. A company had better be certain of the precise benefits—most specifically the payback period—before going ahead and spending huge sums of money on new plant and the latest equipment. Many managers assume that they can obtain a quick payback period on new equipment. This may very well be the case, but there is simply no way you can be confident this will happen until you have tightened your entire operation and then analyzed the cost effectiveness of a new purchase after much of the excess has been removed.

It is a fallacy that one of the basic truths of modern technology and management is that the best way to cut costs is with new plant and equipment. This is absurd. The best way is through the inexpensive methods already described in this book. Only after a company has implemented all of these basic programs, which are certain to save much more than they cost, should any major expenditures for new plant or new equipment be considered. In any overall effort to reduce costs, new plant and equipment should be one of the last considerations, if only because a fundamental concept of real cost reduction is to reduce the people in an operation, not to make the somewhat contradictory decision to purchase new facilities, thereby adding to investment costs and depreciation charges.

Before purchasing a new plant and equipment it is vital that you make certain you are getting the utmost usage out of the plant and equipment the company already owns. During periods of acquisition and consolidation, many top manangers find that they can get three or four times the production from a plant than was the case at the time they inherited it. This increased utilization and productivity can be brought about not only through the use of cost reduction techniques that weed out unneeded personnel, but by improving methods, adding shifts, selling idle or unnecessary equipment, adjusting layout and work flow, and employing the prudent and efficient techniques that good managements should use.

In one actual case history, a division manager was doing $18 million in business and had a 20 percent burden and an 8.6 percent profit. Because sales were accelerating rapidly, he decided to expand into a new plant and purchase new equipment. Suddenly his burden shot up to 28 percent. He has since shut down one of his plants, instituted a comprehensive cost reduction program, and is operating at close to peak efficiency. He is once again in the black.

Some companies are too quick to get rid of aging equipment. When the family car breaks down, the first reaction is to fix it, not to buy a new car. The same instincts should be followed more often in the factory. One large company with which I am familiar has a policy whereby any piece of new equipment is operated as fast and as hard as possible until something breaks down. The failed part is repaired and strengthened, and the process is repeated until another part fails, is strengthened, and repaired again. This process is repeated over and over until the equipment essentially has been custom redesigned and operates at three to four times the manufacturers suggested feeds and speeds or cycle times. This is such a commonsense approach that I often wonder why others don't adopt such a practice. I've come to the conclusion that the U.S. economy is so sales oriented that creative, sound manufacturing practices have fallen into serious decline. Recent business journal articles by some of our most outstanding academicians tend to support this view.

Payback Calculations

Having warned that new plants and equipment are by no means a substitute for good management, one should also realize that there are of course many situations in which a cost analysis reveals the advisability of purchasing new plants and/or equipment. As manufacturing equipment becomes increasingly computerized and automated, the payback period can become shorter and shorter, thereby increasing the likelihood that new purchases will be deemed cost effective.

When trying to decide whether or not to spend large sums of money on new equipment, many companies are satisfied with a payback period of two years. Some companies will accept as many as five years. This is a mistake. The object is to get the biggest bang for your buck. There are enough situations where expenditures for new equipment can pay for itself in one year or less that anything longer is usually unnecessary and unwarranted. I consider a two-year payback period to be the absolute maximum that should be allowed, but basically too long except in rare instances.

In making a cost analysis to determine the amount of time required until new equipment pays for itself, all too often the analysis stops after a simple comparison between the old and new equipment's speed and productivity. This is an important factor, of course, but there are many others to consider as well. For example, the increased efficiency of new equipment will often allow additional volume to be brought in from the outside. Perhaps a previous make-or-buy evaluation concluded that an item could be more profitably puchased from an outside vendor than it could be manufactured internally. Frequently, however, the added capabilities of modern machinery will reduce costs so that the make-or-buy decision can be reevaluated in favor of manufacturing the part in-house. This can reduce burden for all parts, and therefore increase overall sales and profit margins.

Be certain that the new machinery you are purchasing has the flexibility to handle multiple operations. Somewhere down the road you might want to use the new machine to manufacture a similar part, or to make a change in a part you are now manufacturing. The precise nature of future requirements may be unknown, but many new machines are designed with flexibility in mind, an element that in the long run can be extremely valuable. Don't buy machines that cannot perform multiple operations.

Replacing outdated machinery with the latest technology will almost always reduce the total number of machines required in a plant. It is typically a three-to-one relationship; one new machine will replace three old ones. Newer equipment may also eliminate the need for auxiliary machines, such as a hand drill or a small milling device that previously had been kept in a closet until needed. Again, this is a cost savings that is often overlooked when determining the payback period for a particular expenditure.

Be certain also to include the resale value of the old machinery in your payback calculations. Even World War II vintage machinery is usually worth something, even if only for spare parts.

Multi-operation equipment not only reduces the number of total machines that are necessary, but also frees up space and increases inventory turn, since work in process (WIP) is reduced. If a particular part is currently manufactured in four or five separate operations by four or five different machines, there is considerable down time, or work in process, when a part is sitting idle, waiting to be moved on to the next machine. But the latest generation of machines can frequently manufacture the part in one fluid operation, thereby increasing efficiency and reducing its per unit cost.

Replacing several machines with one new machine will also reduce a plant's square footage requirements. This too might alter a previously-made make-or-buy evaluation, or even enable an entire plant to be closed or consolidated.

Exhibit 11–2 New Plant and Equipment Example

A $100 million company manufactures high precision stainless steel machine parts. $2 million is spent for new machinery. The number of persons required for the operation is initially reduced from 123 to 79, and the number of machine tools is reduced from 80 to 48. Not only do the 48 machines do the work of 80 with 44 fewer workers, but 1,600,000 parts, or the equivalent of about 44,000 standard hours, that were being farmed out are now able to be moved back in house. The fewer pieces of machinery drop the operation's square footage requirement, and a sister plant is able to be closed and consolidated into this plant. Nineteen months later the new equipment has paid for itself. Phase II is ready to begin. A repeat of Phase I, it will bring the number of persons in the machine shop down under 40, while reducing through-put time to a fraction of what it was.

The New Industrial Revolution

Deciding whether or not to purchase new equipment has become more complex in recent years, as we have entered what might be termed a new industrial revolution, the effects of which we have only begun to witness. A few years from now machines that today are tape controlled will be voice controlled. They will be tended by robots who ultimately will have vision. The only people on the manufacturing floor will be setup personnel and service technicans. In the very near future, factories will be operated on a seven-day, three-shift basis, while they will be manned only for one shift for five days. The various machines will run automatically and shut off when the job is either completed or requires a tooling change. In some plants around the country this kind of revolutionary situation has already arrived in machining, welding, painting, sheet metal, and some assembly areas. Already many plants have islands of automation. We're at a point now where an engineering program comes off the computer and goes automatically to the machines. We call it DCC, or direct computer control.

The factory of the future probably will be totally controlled by a microprocessor, which will be capable not only of running the entire manufacturing operation automatically, but also of furnishing an instant evaluation of inventory, a cost reduction tool in itself. Work in process inventories will be reduced, as will "floor to floor" time. Instead of the bustle of human activity within a huge industrial complex associated with the factory of yesterday, a few workers wearing white coats and probably on salary will calmly oversee the operation, walking quietly through a much smaller building. Meanwhile, from their homes or small suburban centers, office workers will be able to operate word processors tied to central computers.

While it is true that we are in the midst of a major technological revolution, the cost of shifting over to this new equipment will be staggering, and obsolescence from ongoing state-of-the-art advancements will be rapid. Nevertheless, the potential cost savings are enormous. Not only will savings result from a decrease in direct and indirect labor and fringes, but equally important savings will result from such things as the reduction of required square footage, much lower scrap, longer running times, automatic feeds, and a much more rapid processing of inventory.

Aside from technological advancements, there are at least three other factors that will continue to hasten this new industrial revolution:

1. *The cost of labor has skyrocketed during the past two decades.* Not only have wages increased dramatically, but fringe benefits have taken an increasingly larger percentage of the total cost of labor. Check your factory burden to see what percentage is made up of fringe costs; it is substantial—probably in the neighborhood of 40 percent.

2. *The population of the United States is aging.* Demographic experts tell us that in the near future there will not be nearly as many people entering the work force as there were in previous generations. Factory employment as we know it today just won't be attractive to coming generations.

3. *The productivity of the American worker is steadily declining.* At the same time the productivity of robots has increased, humans have been moving in the opposite direction. Holidays, coffee breaks, vacations, sick days, personal days, and increased tardiness and absenteeism all have worked against productivity output per employee.

Remember, however, that until this revolution conclusively convinces your financial department that large expenditures for the latest in plant and equipment will guarantee a short payback period, you should not be led astray by what are often the empty promises of shiny new equipment. The bottom line in any industrial endeavor is profit, and the finest plant and equipment in the world will not guarantee it. In more cases than is generally realized, big outlays for new plant and equipment increase burden to a point where it offsets all or a major portion of the profit it produces. (We already have discussed in Chapter 4 the problems of generating enough money just for working capital, let alone long-term investment.)

Putting it another way, although we are indeed in the midst of an exciting revolution, companies should not act too precipitously. The other side of the coin, however, is that those who fail to investigate and begin to participate in this new industrial revolution are going to be left behind and will have difficulty surviving. Experiment with the new equipment before committing large sums of money. If you have implemented all the cost reduction and profit improvement techniques discussed in this handbook, you could have the available funds to purchase this new equipment. Make certain you know what you are getting into and act prudently. It is an old adage but an accurate one: "Act in haste and repent at leisure."

Remember above all else that it is through careful and constant maintenance of a comprehensive cost reduction program that better profits are realized. Regardless of the future capability of robots and other technological advancements, the less expensive cost reduction techniques we have discussed will be more necessary than ever during the remaining years of this century as a predicted shortfall of capital formation makes it more difficult to buy new equipment and to build new structures.

The manager who now knows how to get peak usage from existing facilities and personnel will be the one most likely to understand and adopt the new techniques described here. We have one more chance in America. It lies in tape-controlled machines, robots, and the use of small employee/management groups to communicate within the organization. But it also lies with instituting better management techniques, which includes implementing the applicable cost reduction program outlined in this text. This is the reason why *The Harry Figgie Guide to Cost Reduction and Profit Improvement* was written.

12

Conclusion

Perhaps a final chapter should have been added to this guide entitled "Maintaining Cost Reduction as a Continuing Priority." The chapter could have consisted of one sentence only: "Now turn to page 1 and begin your cost reduction program again."

The temptation after cutting costs by 10 to 15 percent or more is to feel satisfied that your company is now operating at peak efficiency and maximum profitability. This is a fallacy and is as unrealistic as it is costly. Without continued maintenance, such things as excess personnel, wasteful habits, and countless other inefficiencies will begin to creep back into your operation within a remarkably short period of time. For this reason, and because no cost reduction program can eliminate all the unnecessary fat the first time around, you will be surprised to find that significant reductions in costs can be made year after year, no matter how many years a cost reduction program has been followed. Even in a well-run operation, an ongoing comprehensive cost reduction program should save you an additional 4 to 5 percent annually, each and every year.

When presented with the kind of comprehensive cost reduction effort outlined in the previous pages, many presidents may feel ill-equipped to implement every one of the techniques by themselves. Presidents who have come up the ranks through purchasing, for example, may not feel sufficiently familiar with the engineering department to determine whether there are underutilized technicians who could be reassigned to another, understaffed department. The normal reaction may then be to charge the engineering manager with the responsibility of recommending where cuts should be made in that department.

This is fine. But what happens when your engineering manager comes back and tells you that the engineering department is operating at 100 percent efficiency and that it would be impossible to streamline the operation? Now the monkey has returned to your back. You may have to resort to making it clear that overhead *is* too high, and telling your head of engineering that if he or she does not submit specific cost reduction recommendations, an across-the-board manpower reduction will have to be implemented. This should prompt the department manager to take another look at the situation.

I know of one instance where a manager told a company president that his staff was working at 110 percent efficiency and there was no possible way any cuts could be made. The president responded by suggesting they walk directly to that manager's department and perform an immediate informal work sampling. The president told the manager that if at that moment every one of his employees were busy performing his or her designated task, his department would not have to implement the "quick and dirty" cost saving measures outlined in the first three chapters of this book. The manager was suddenly much more cooperative.

Even after you receive recommendations from your department heads, it is then important to coordinate the cost reduction effort, perhaps by holding one or more meetings to which all department heads attend. It is your job to take a look at the total picture. If you pass this responsibility down to your subordinates, you are going to lose the synergism of picking up savings between departments. With everyone sitting around the table, it is your job to ask, "Are there any combined savings that can be implemented?" One department may have a person who is only being effective half the time, but is nevertheless vital to the operation. A similar situation may exist in another department, in which case two half-time jobs, currently being performed by two persons, could be altered so that they both are filled by one employee. Two or more executives might be able to share a secretary, for example. In other words, the savings of the whole might be greater that the pieces. Effective communications is the key here.

A Company-Wide Effort

Cost reduction must be more than a regimented program of rules and procedures. Cost cutting measures become truly successful not only through an organized, comprehensive, continuing program, but also by making cost reduction a top priority—a way of life. The importance of cost reduction must be truly understood not only by yourself, but by every salaried employee from the top down.

Day after day, week after week, year after year, your company must not only implement such specific programs as organizational and ratio analysis, work sampling, product redesign, value analysis, labor standards, and proper purchasing techniques, but must also continually be ready to thwart the many routine business practices that tend to encourage waste. Your company must, for example, make certain almost on a daily basis that its pricing structure is not giving away all (or more) of the savings that have been gained through cost reduction (Chapter 10), that appropriate emphasis is being placed on the purchasing department (Chapter 6), and that costly and capital intensive growth is not replacing more cost effective internal measures (Chapter 4).

There is a medium-sized company with which I am familiar that truly exemplifies how a modern, cost-conscious corporation should behave. By its daily actions it is clear that this company recognizes the direct relationship between reducing costs and improving profitability, as well as the vital necessity of making cost reduction an ongoing top priority. This company manufactures approximately 1,500 different product lines and employs about 300 people, 25 percent of whom are engineers. They stringently follow the cost reduction guidelines outlined in this guide. They also have gone far beyond these techniques by developing an innovative, creative cost reduction system of their own. Perhaps most important, their top executives, particularly the president, have for many years made cost reduction a top priority for each and every one of the company's salaried employees. Reducing costs has become second nature to the people at this company. Indeed, every year their projected budget includes a planned 4 percent reduction in costs. This target is met or exceeded year in and year out.

In briefly outlining this particular company's outstanding approach and commitment to cost reduction, it is important to keep in mind that the specifics of its program are not nearly as crucial as the fact that it has made cost reduction a continuing top priority. Another company might organize its cost reduction effort in a completely different manner, but as long as it has an overall commitment to the procedures outlined in this text, substantial cost savings will result.

The theory behind this company's approach to cost reduction is that the many people responsible for the various details of an industrial operation are in the best position to suggest and implement cost savings in their respective areas. These men and women know better than anyone else about their particular job functions. This company makes a concerted effort to extract that knowledge and implement it in a way that reduces costs.

Their cost reduction strategy is really quite simple. As a condition of employment, every salaried worker must submit cost reduction suggestions that are studied, accepted, and implemented. Every salaried employee is assigned to a cost reduction team. Salary increases are directly related to an employee's cost reduction contributions. All suggestions must be submitted in writing, using the form presented in Exhibit 12-1. The program insists upon 100 percent participation. In fact, in all the years it has been implemented, only one salaried employee chose not to participate, thereby choosing not to be employed by this firm.

Although some jobs, such as engineering and purchasing, are of course more conducive to cost reduction than others, no job is immune. In a typical year this company's sixty salaried employees submit five hundred cost reduction proposals. Some people submit as many as twenty proposals, while other suggestions are submitted jointly by more than one employee.

The cost reduction ideas range widely in both scope and substance. It is the *attitude* that is important, not the amount of money involved, although the overall company goal is of course to reduce costs by as much as possible. But the real goal is to encourage all employees to persistently and continually think of ways in which costs can be reduced in their area of employment.

Exhibits 12–2, 12–3, and 12–4 offer three examples of the many cost reduction suggestions submitted.

Exhibit 12–1 Cost Improvement Docket

TOTAL ESTIMATED SAVINGS (ANNUALIZED)		DOCKET NO.	
COST OF IMPLEMENTING DOCKET		DEPARTMENT NO.	
ANNUAL NET SAVINGS		DATE	
TYPE OF DOCKET:		SUBMITTED BY:	
		APPROVED BY:	
PRODUCT ☐ MANAGED ☐		APPROVED BY:	

DESCRIPTION:

ASSIGNMENT OF RESPONSIBILITY			
DATE	ASSIGNED TO	SCHEDULE OF ACTIVITY	RESULTS

THIS DOCKET IS: DATE _____
☐ APPROVED FOR _____
☐ DROPPED BECAUSE _____

Exhibit 12–2 Cost Improvement Docket Example 1

TOTAL ESTIMATED SAVINGS (ANNUALIZED)	$1,200	DOCKET NO.	
COST OF IMPLEMENTING DOCKET	0	DEPARTMENT NO.	Sales
ANNUAL NET SAVINGS	$1,200	DATE	
TYPE OF DOCKET:		SUBMITTED BY:	
		APPROVED BY:	
PRODUCT ☐ MANAGED ☒		APPROVED BY:	

DESCRIPTION:

When making airplane reservations for Mr. W. to travel
to Los Angeles, I applied the Senior Citizen Special
Rate and obtained a 33 percent discount. The total
cost of the ticket without the Senior Citizen discount
is $718.00. The total cost of the ticket with the 33
percent Senior Citizen discount is $478.00, a total
savings of $240.00. The estimated annual savings would
be five times this amount.

ASSIGNMENT OF RESPONSIBILITY			
DATE	ASSIGNED TO	SCHEDULE OF ACTIVITY	RESULTS

Exhibit 12–3 Cost Improvement Docket Example 2

TOTAL ESTIMATED SAVINGS (ANNUALIZED)	$11,266	DOCKET NO.	
COST OF IMPLEMENTING DOCKET		DEPARTMENT NO.	
ANNUAL NET SAVINGS		DATE	
TYPE OF DOCKET:		SUBMITTED BY:	
		APPROVED BY:	
PRODUCT ☑ MANAGED ☐		APPROVED BY:	

DESCRIPTION:

By unitizing test leads for

a product into a single fixture,

20 minutes per unit is saved during

adjustment and final testing.

Originally, test leads were connected

individually in such a way that

a short would be probable.

Total units = 5,633 units

20 minutes/unit = 1877.67 hours × $6/hour = $11,266

ASSIGNMENT OF RESPONSIBILITY			
DATE	ASSIGNED TO	SCHEDULE OF ACTIVITY	RESULTS

THIS DOCKET IS: DATE _____
☐ APPROVED FOR _____
☐ DROPPED BECAUSE _____

Exhibit 12–4 Cost Improvement Docket Example 3

TOTAL ESTIMATED SAVINGS (ANNUALIZED)	$19,069.88
COST OF IMPLEMENTING DOCKET	
ANNUAL NET SAVINGS	$19,069.88
TYPE OF DOCKET:	
PRODUCT ☒ MANAGED ☐	

DOCKET NO.	
DEPARTMENT NO.	Engineering
DATE	
SUBMITTED BY:	
APPROVED BY:	
APPROVED BY:	

DESCRIPTION: Change terminals in B3 series bases to one piece, removing two part numbers from stock. Terminals can not be torqued out of base.

Part numbers removed	$1.29 per base part savings $818.40
35180-1 3 per 1.16 each	Removing two part numbers $50.00
35400-1 3 per .36 each	Scrap rate 40% 15,265.80
1.52 each / × 3	Base labor saving 20 minutes 163.68
4.56 per base	Line labor saving 2 hours 2772.00
35177-1 6 per .22 each	$19,069.88
35401-1 6 per .24 each	
1.01 / × 6 / $6.06	

ASSIGNMENT OF RESPONSIBILITY			
DATE	ASSIGNED TO	SCHEDULE OF ACTIVITY	RESULTS

THIS DOCKET IS: DATE_____
☐ APPROVED FOR _____
☐ DROPPED BECAUSE _____

As is apparent, the examples are quite different from one other. Exhibit 12–2, for example, submitted by a secretary, involves reducing the cost of air travel. The annual savings of $1,200 is in this case an estimate, since the actual savings will depend on the amount of travel undertaken by Mr. W.

Exhibits 12–3 and 12–4 are product changes, as opposed to Exhibit 12–2 which was a management operations change. Exhibit 12–3 was submitted by a foreman and resulted in a performance improvement, as well as a time saving, and thus a cost savings. Exhibit 12–4 was submitted by an engineer and involved consolidating two pieces of a product's component into one.

This company's cost reduction program is administered by the head of purchasing, a recognition in itself of one of the most important cost reduction tenets: purchasing is usually the area where the greatest cost savings can be realized.

Every salaried employee is in turn assigned to a cost reduction team, headed by a team captain. It is the responsibility of each team to make certain that all members participate in cost reduction. They have found that the teams allow for convenient discussion and analysis of cost reduction suggestions before they are submitted. It is noteworthy that the same theory and techniques that have proven so successful in the formation of quality circles can be utilized within cost reduction teams. As a further illustration of the cost reduction team concept, Exhibit 12–5 (page 203) presents an organizational chart of this division's eight cost reduction teams, and Appendix III lists the major elements of participation.

Exhibit 12–6 (page 204) summarizes this division's cost improvement program for one recent year. As you can see, all eight teams contributed, and the company surpassed its goal of $550,000, which represents approximately 4 percent of total sales. Awards are given to the individuals and teams with the most cost improvement success. More importantly, an employee's cost reduction contribution is the single most important factor during salary review.

Exhibit 12–6 shows that purchasing and engineering are two of the largest cost reductions contributors. This is to be expected since these are the two areas with the most control over expensive material costs. It is interesting, however, that marketing was the second largest contributor, and the controller's department was fourth. Marketing's job is to move the product, not necessarily to cut costs. By the same token, the controller's department, while adept at numbers, traditionally does not make the creative decisions necessary to reduce costs. This company's team rankings, however, demonstrate that substantial savings are possible from all departments. *Everyone* can and should be involved.

There is no reason why the cost reduction/profit improvement program that has proven so successful for so many years at this company cannot be implemented in every manufacturing firm in the United States. It is neither complicated nor costly. The program is simply a commitment to the many profit improvement techniques detailed in this text, and a recognition that all employees, regardless of their functions, are aware of ways in which costs can easily be reduced or avoided. If all employees—and this philosophy absolutely must be telegraphed from the top down—make certain that proper attention is paid to reducing costs whenever and wherever possible, the benefits to the company will be enormous.

Exhibit 12–5 Cost Reduction Teams

1
1. Superintendent, Machine Shop
2. Foreman
3. Foreman

2
1. Supervisor, Assembly Depts.
2. Foreman
3. Foreman
4. Foreman
5. Expeditor
6. Foreman
7. Foreman
8. Foreman
9. Jr. Engineer

3
1. Supervisor, Process Engineer
2. Process Engineer
3. Maintenance Foreman

4
1. Purchasing Manager
2. Senior Buyer
3. Secretary
4. Foreman, Quality Assurance

5
1. Manufacturing Manager
2. Supervisor, Storeroom
3. Keypunch Operator
4. Production Planner
5. Production Scheduler
6. Computer Operator

7. Keypunch Operator
8. Production Scheduler
9. Supervisor, Data Processing

6
1. Engineering Manager
2. Engineering Data Coordinator
3. Supervisor, Drafting
4. Draftsman
5. Project Engineer
6. Project Engineer
7. Project Engineer
8. Project Engineer
9. Project Engineer
10. Engineering Section Manager
11. Design Engineer
12. Jr. Engineer
13. Supervisor, Test Dept.
14. Jr. Engineer
15. Jr. Engineer
16. Jr. Engineer
17. Jr. Engineer
18. Secretary

7
1. V.P. Marketing
2. Contracts Manager
3. Supervisor, Order Service
4. Sales Engineer
5. Customer Service Agent
6. Executive Secretary
7. Secretary
8. Sales Engineer

8
1. Controller
2. Secretary
3. Secretary
4. Jr. Accountant

Exhibit 12–6 Cost Improvement Docket Summary

TEAM NO.		CHAIRMAN				GOAL	$550,000.00	YEAR TO DATE		
		PROPOSED		COST AVOIDANCE		DROPPED		COMPLETED		
NO.	NAME	PRODUCT	MANAGED	PRODUCT	MANAGED	PRODUCT	MANAGED	PRODUCT	MANAGED	TOTAL
1	Superintendent, Machine Shop	3	7					3	7	$49,340
2	Supervisor, Assembly Depts.	32	13					32	13	$43,157
3	Supervisor, Process Engineering	15	5					15	5	$2,401
4	Purchasing Manager	8	36					8	36	$81,524
5	Production Control Supervisor	67	4					67	4	$13,499
6	Engineering Manager	53	29					53	29	$193,609
7	V.P. Marketing	18	58					18	58	$130,765
8	Controller	—	29					—	29	$71,175
TOTAL		196	181					196	181	$585,470

Appendixes

Appendix I:

Work Sampling

Although the basic theory of work sampling is rather simple, some of the specifics of its operation can seem complicated. For this reason, Appendix I has been prepared to expound upon some of the sampling theories outlined in Chapter 2, and to furnish many of the definitions of productive and nonproductive work status in an actual work sampling procedure.

Exhibit A-1 demonstrates that in observing the operation of a particular machine that your records indicate should have, say, a 73 percent productive occurrence, you know in advance, from the statistics of the law of probability, that you can obtain accuracy to within ± 3 percent if you make 1,640 observations. The 73 percent productive occurrence is simply an estimate of the percentage of time that the work place to be sampled is operating at an acceptable productive pace.

Note that Exhibit A-1 tells you that 145 observations will provide a ± 10 percent accuracy. Usually, however, ± 5 percent is acceptable, which in this case would necessitate 590 observations. This is invaluable information to have when, at a later date, you wish to check up on the operation of that machine to see that it is being utilized at the rate that has been prescribed for it.

Although there are many different ways to use Exhibit A-2, probably the simplest method is to set up a chart similar to the one illustrated in Exhibit A-3. This example assumes that each observation tour will take thirty minutes to complete. You will also want to vary the time of the first tour, so that the first employee surveyed will not always be observed on the half-hour. The times on some days therefore might be

Exhibit A-1 Probability of Work Sampling Accuracy

Percent of Total Time Occupied by Activity	±1	±2	±3	±4	±5	±6	±7	±8	±9	(±10)
60	26,670	6,670	2,960	1,670	1,070	740	545	415	330	265
61	25,570	6,390	2,840	1,600	1,020	710	520	400	315	255
62	24,520	6,130	2,720	1,560	980	680	500	385	305	245
63	23,490	5,870	2,610	1,470	940	650	480	365	290	235
64	22,500	5,680	2,500	1,440	900	625	460	350	275	225
65	21,540	5,300	2,390	1,350	860	600	440	335	265	215
66	20,610	5,150	2,290	1,290	825	570	420	320	255	205
67	19,700	4,925	2,190	1,230	790	545	400	305	245	195
68	18,820	4,705	2,080	1,180	750	520	385	295	230	190
69	17,970	4,460	2,000	1,120	720	500	365	280	220	180
70	17,140	4,280	1,900	1,070	685	475	350	265	210	170
71	16,840	4,085	1,815	1,020	655	455	335	255	200	165
72	15,560	3,830	1,730	970	620	430	315	245	190	155
73	14,760	3,700	1,640	925	590	410	300	230	180	145
74	14,050	3,510	1,560	880	560	390	285	220	175	140
75	13,330	3,380	1,480	835	535	370	270	210	165	135
76	12,630	3,160	1,400	790	505	350	255	195	155	125
77	11,950	2,900	1,330	745	490	330	245	185	145	120
78	11,280	2,820	1,250	705	450	315	230	175	140	110
79	10,630	2,600	1,180	665	425	295	215	165	130	105
80	10,000	2,500	1,150	625	400	275	205	155	125	100
81	9,580	2,340	1,040	585	375	260	190	145	115	94
82	8,780	2,195	975	550	350	235	180	135	110	88
83	8,190	2,050	940	510	325	225	165	130	100	83
84	7,620	1,960	845	475	295	210	155	120	94	76
85	7,060	1,760	785	440	280	195	145	110	87	71
86	6,510	1,630	725	405	260	180	130	100	80	65
87	5,950	1,490	665	375	240	165	120	95	74	60
88	5,450	1,360	605	340	220	150	110	85	67	55
89	4,940	1,280	550	310	200	135	100	77	61	49
90	4,440	1,110	490	280	175	125	90	69	55	44
91	3,960	990	440	250	160	110	80	62	49	40
92	3,480	870	385	220	140	96	70	51	45	35
93	3,010	750	350	190	120	83	61	47	37	30
94	2,550	640	265	150	100	71	52	40	31	26
95	2,110	525	220	130	85	59	43	33	26	21
96	1,670	420	185	105	67	46	34	26	21	17
97	1,240	310	140	78	50	34	25	19	15	12
98	815	205	91	51	33	23	17	15	10	8
99	405	100	45	23	16	11	8	6	5	4

8:05, 8:35, 9:05, 9:35,...; on other days 8:10, 8:40, 9:10, 9:40,.... The code should begin 01, 02....

Referring now to the random number table in Exhibit A-2, proceed vertically down each column in turn and select the first five numbers that correspond to one of the time codes in Exhibit A-3. Note that the first number from Exhibit A-2 that corresponds to a code designated in Exhibit A-3 is 07, which is 11:00 A.M. The next is 04, which is 9:30 A.M.

Exhibit A-2 Table of Two-Digit Random Numbers[*]

98 78 82 54 47	20 83 80 10 41	35 22 23 03 98	79 74 41 35 03
78 58 68 87 41	11 08 81 29 89	71 23 10 01 79	25 06 00 45 80
51 42 21 03 88	20 05 35 93 00	68 12 09 55 09	36 54 95 22 82
93 15 07 60 86	67 37 94 24 35	82 44 19 92 96	21 84 29 04 29
27 (12) 31 66 62	09 54 17 31 23	27 30 37 36 79	75 50 39 57 12
79 44 83 55 47	96 50 93 56 82	58 16 35 18 87	64 08 22 47 93
89 73 43 91 03	57 91 35 40 64	13 61 94 37 16	09 93 96 25 87
29 30 90 00 58	15 99 93 33 67	80 08 59 21 66	13 54 56 85 25
97 33 17 26 25	04 73 18 10 05	34 40 32 65 07	28 68 29 31 97
07 15 44 92 47	28 50 93 03 53	37 70 19 68 59	95 39 87 90 46
82 50 34 50 80	23 67 81 25 02	83 08 12 80 00	25 31 33 80 06
59 21 86 16 30	27 85 16 26 34	50 15 87 22 69	71 36 95 90 76
04 19 60 33 05	29 02 33 74 56	38 84 21 07 35	93 54 70 18 47
96 91 44 09 94	06 89 50 88 83	82 50 11 82 51	30 68 91 06 28
31 71 03 53 38	94 02 52 72 05	44 49 53 42 43	00 36 97 67 64
03 70 22 67 59	98 10 64 68 08	79 06 89 48 41	85 72 10 87 24
08 45 79 46 89	74 73 67 60 15	70 37 61 44 07	67 89 81 54 26
37 80 05 75 64	48 51 68 68 27	71 75 45 32 27	76 35 26 58 88
90 63 56 69 37	19 74 48 63 31	52 36 48 40 66	72 66 03 41 87
22 69 38 02 88	89 71 43 01 87	41 79 42 99 29	41 08 47 32 19
05 79 69 67 64	36 14 82 65 26	40 51 63 42 48	85 48 34 12 04
48 (01) 53 03 82	64 24 06 31 03	97 44 82 24 89	88 48 66 54 10
94 64 97 27 25	62 23 94 40 54	56 32 97 78 90	58 86 41 75 19
(15) 85 82 52 08	52 96 26 92 88	93 11 03 23 52	78 23 57 85 43
(09) 81 37 66 56	99 08 59 19 48	29 69 21 64 95	12 08 15 24 45
43 83 99 02 76	12 16 45 52 66	35 70 93 09 52	75 40 34 35 62
31 98 09 80 62	75 26 64 57 26	46 41 47 90 97	99 46 10 51 42
81 35 42 62 84	37 02 59 78 16	17 96 05 71 39	88 05 34 05 92
97 95 56 39 75	65 47 61 86 33	17 88 55 33 69	70 87 79 94 46
37 63 35 93 23	17 30 14 51 51	17 28 21 74 67	12 11 57 19 27
39 22 96 00 48	52 49 62 09 40	08 30 27 54 70	96 06 52 12 80
61 29 84 34 51	60 19 77 82 16	64 45 02 27 04	65 55 90 95 04
38 84 18 10 29	19 90 66 06 73	37 09 60 50 21	52 72 01 52 70
64 29 48 04 08	55 72 25 25 77	54 26 27 24 39	66 67 06 40 00
64 (02) 32 99 63	62 42 89 32 20	81 14 08 40 45	22 15 37 49 38

[*]For underscore, see Exhibit A-4; for circle see Exhibit A-5

Exhibit A-3 Coding Observation Times

Time	Code	Time	Code
8:00 A.M.	01	12:30	09
8:30 A.M.	02	1:00	10
9:00 A.M.	03	1:30	11
9:30 A.M.	04	2:00	12
10:00 A.M.	05	2:30	13
10:30 A.M.	06	3:00	14
11:00 A.M.	07	3:30	15
11:30 A.M.	08	4:00	16
Lunch		4:30	17

Exhibit A-4 Selecting Random Observation Times (First Day)

Random Number	Sample Time
03	9:00 A.M.
04	9:30 A.M.
05	10:00 A.M.
07	11:00 A.M.
08	11:30 A.M.

The example given in Exhibit A-4 assumes that five tours are required each day. If more tours are required, simply select more random numbers from Exhibit A-2. This process should be repeated for each day of the work sampling by continuing to proceed down the columns of random numbers.

Clearly, however, there is something wrong with Exhibit A-4. Using the formula we have described, all our tours occur in the morning, not a very scientific or accurate method, one might think. But the laws of probability protect us. Exhibit A-4 has selected only the times of the tours for the first day of the work sampling operation. The next day another five tours are selected using the same method.

Exhibit A-5 was compiled by continuing down the columns of Exhibit A-2, beginning where we left off after compiling Exhibit A-4. A number from the random number table is used only once within each tour, so 15 is skipped after it appears the first time.

Note that this time we have come up with three observations in the afternoon and two in the morning, a much more equitable distribution.

You can be assured that over the entire run of your work sampling operation this kind of equitable distribution between morning and afternoon will be maintained. Remember also that the tours should not always begin on the half-hour. Exhibit A-5 therefore might actually read 8:05, 8:35, 12:35, 2:05, and 3:35. You might then want the tours on the third day to begin ten minutes after the hour, the fourth day fifteen minutes after the hour, and so on.

Exhibit A-5 Selecting Random Observation Times (Second Day)

Random Number	Sample Time
01	8:00 A.M.
02	8:30 A.M.
09	12:30 P.M.
12	2:00 P.M.
15	3:30 P.M.

You must decide at the outset how many times each day you will visit and observe any one particular work center. Let us assume that your sampling tables indicate a visit ten times daily. You will do it at random, taking extreme care not to follow a set pattern. If the machines are located in one common area, you might observe what is happening at as many as fifty machines in the space of five minutes, ten minutes at most.

The procedure is to record what is happening to each machine at the precise instant that it comes into the observer's view on each visit. At the end of ten days, one-hundred observations of each machine will have been made, provided your ten-times-a-day observation schedule has been maintained. Your record on a particular machine might look like Exhibit A-6.

Exhibit A-6 Work Sampling Observation Chart

Element	Observations	Percent of Total
Operation	62	62
Setup	18	18
Maintenance	10	10
Delay	8	8
Total	100	100

The percentage of total will vary, of course, as more observations are made, but from this small sampling there is in all probability a delay ratio of 8 percent on this one machine. Too much time also appears to be spent on maintenance. How do you verify this analysis? No problem. Make observations of other similar machines, and keep making observations! When danger signals such as this arise, pick up the pace of observations say to twenty a day, or more. But even if you don't increase the number of daily observations, the accuracy of your sampling will increase with the passage of time, as long as the regular number of observations is maintained.

Exhibits A-7, A-8, and A-9 show work sampling definitions that should be recorded for absenteeism, productive work status, and nonproductive work status. These definitions should be used when recording observations on a Factory Work Observation Sheet, such as the one depicted in Exhibit A-10.

Exhibit A-11 offers office productivity definitions to be used in Exhibit A-12, a work sampling form for office observations. Exhibit A-13 is a pace rate sampling form, and Exhibit A-14 provides machine utilization definitions for Exhibit A-15, a sample observation sheet for a machine utilization survey.

Exhibit A-7 Work Sampling Absenteeism Cosde

Code	Reason
A	Vacation or leave of absence.
B	Out of plant, personal business (sick, dentist, doctor, etc.).
C	Out of plant, company business.
D	Late to work.
E	Transferred to another classification or department. (Indicate department or classification.)

Exhibit A-8 Productive Factory Definitions

1. Operator productive at work station; operator working at stations, e.g., loading fixture.

2. Operator handling material at work station in the normal course of duties, e.g., loading and unloading machine.

3. Operator walking at work station; in transit within confines of work station while performing prescribed duties.

4. Machine cycle time: operator idle while machine performs operation. (Too much idleness, however, may mean that the operator could use a second machine.)

5. Rework: operator repairing or correcting a prior operation. (As rework operations are difficult to identify, operators should be provided with red tags and instructed to display them prominently when performing rework.)

6. Training: foreman and/or operator instructing another employee, and employee being trained.

7. Material handling: operator handling material outside the confines of assigned work center.

8. Talk: a supervisor talking with person in his or her span of control; operator talking with supervisor.

9. Supervisor working at desk.

Exhibit A-9 Nonproductive Factory Definitions

1. Waiting: when an operator appears to be waiting, the observer should determine the reason and record it as follows: (a) Material (b) Job assignment (c) Setup (d) Crane (e) Quality control (f) Maintenance (g) Engineering.

2. Personal/Idle: operator idle for no apparent reason or on break if breaks are being sampled.

3. Talk: operator talking with individual other than supervisor.

4. Walk: empty-handed operator in transit for any reason.

5. Telephone: any time spent on the telephone.

Exhibit A-10 Factory Work Observation Sheet

Division _____ Dept. _____ Class. _____

PRODUCTIVE									Total obser-vations	% occ.
At station										
Material handled—station										
Walk at station										
Machine cycling										
Setup										
Rework										
Training										
Material handling										
Talk business with supervisor										
Supervisor at desk										
TOTAL PRODUCTIVE										
% PRODUCTIVE										
NONPRODUCTIVE										
Wait—Material										
Wait—Job assignment										
Wait—Setup										
Wait—Crane										
Wait—Quality control										
Wait—Maintenance										
Wait—Engineering										
Personal/Idle										
Talk business										
Walk empty										
Telephone										
Subtotal Observations Away										
Total Attended Observations										

Calculations

A	Raw % productive	
B	Delay allowances	
C	Revised % productive	
	A ± B = C	
D	% Pace	
E	% Personal, Fatigue & Delay	
F	Nonproductive Index	
	C × D × E = F	
G	Optimum required	
	J × F = G	
H	Variance	
	J − G = H	
I	Excess Employment Maximum	
	N − G = I	
J	Study employees	
N	Payroll	

Exhibit A-11 Productive and Nonproductive Office Definitions

Office—Productive

1. Work at desk, write: individual writing at desk.

2. Work at desk, other; other work performed at individual's desk.

3. Work in department: productive work performed in an individual's assigned department but away from desk.

4. Work out of department: productive work performed outside an individual's assigned department.

5. Filing at desk: insertion/retrieval of files at individual's desk.

6. Filing in department: insertion/retrieval of files within an individual's assigned department.

7. Filing out of department: insertion/retrieval of files outside an individual's assigned department.

8. Typing: self-explanatory.

9. Dictating: self-explanatory.

10. Taking dictation: self-explanatory.

11. Talk in department: individual talking business with another individual in assigned department. Supervisor talking to individual within his or her span of control.

12. Talk out of department: individual or supervisor talking business with another individual outside assigned department.

13. Telephone: any time spent on the telephone.

14. Apparent thinking: individual who appears to be thinklng.

15. Transport material: individual walking with material.

16. Meeting: group of individuals in conference.

Office—Nonproductive

1. Personal/Idle: individual idle for no apparent reason or on break if breaks are being sampled.

2. Walk empty: empty-handed individual in transit for any reason.

3. Wait for: when an individual appears to be waiting, the observer should determine the reason and record it as follows: (a) Copy machine (b) Information or material (c) Individual.

Exhibit A-12 Office Work Observation Sheet

Division _____ Dept. _____ Class. _____

PRODUCTIVE										Total obser-vations	% occ.
Work—desk—write											
Work—desk—other											
Work in dept.											
Work out of dept.											
Filing—Desk											
Filing—Dept.											
Filing—Out of Dept.											
Typing											
Dictation											
Taking dictation											
Talk business in dept. to sup.											
Talk business out of dept.											
Telephone											
Apparent thinking											
Transporting material											
Meeting											
TOTAL PRODUCTIVE											
% PRODUCTIVE											
NONPRODUCTIVE											
Personal/Idle											
Walk empty											
Wait—Copy machine											
Wait info, mail											
Wait—Individual											
Subtotal Observations Away											
Total Attended Observations											

Calculations

A	Raw % productive	
B	Delay allowances	
C	Revised % productive	
	A + B = C	
D	% Pace	
E	% Personal, Fatigue & Delay	
F	Nonproductive Index	
	C × D × E = F	
G	Optimum required	
	J × F = G	
H	Variance	
	J − G = H	
I	Excess Employment Maximum	
	N − G = I	
J	Study employees	
N	Payroll	

Exhibit A-13 Work Sampling Pace Rate Summary

Rate	Dept. J.C.	Dept. J.C.	Dept. J.C.	Dept. J.C.	Dept. J.C.	Dept. J.C.	Dept. J.C.	Dept. J.C.	Dept. J.C.	Dept. J.C.	Dept. J.C.	Dept. J.C.
60												
70												
80												
90												
100												
110												
120												
130												
TOTAL OBSERVATIONS												
LEVELED OBSERVATIONS												
% PACE												

Exhibit A-14 Machine Utilization Definitions

Productive

- Running/Cycling—machine is running or cycling and producing.

- Load/Unload—machine is idle while operator prepares product for operation or removes product after completion of operation.

- Setup—machine is idle while operator tears down previous setup or prepares new setup.

Nonproductive

- Not scheduled—machine is not scheduled for operation.

- Load/Unload—machine has broken down or malfunctioned.

- Idle/Other—machine is idle for unexplained reason or reason not covered above.

The preceding definitions of productive and nonproductive work time have been provided as examples only. The precise nature of any work sampling operation will vary according to your company's requirements and according to the particular experience of the industrial engineer or outside consultant whom you hire to direct it.

Exhibit A-15 Machine Utilization Survey—Observation Sheet

Division _____ Dept. _____ Date _____

	PRODUCTIVE			NON-PRODUCTIVE					PRODUCTIVE			NON-PRODUCTIVE			
Tag No.	Running Cycling	Loading Unloading	Setup	Idle Other	Idle Break-down	Not Sched-uled	Total Obser-vations	Tag No.	Running Cycling	Loading Unloading	Setup	Idle Other	Idle Break-down	Not Sched-uled	Total Obser-vations
1								26							
2								27							
3								28							
4								29							
5								30							
6								31							
7								32							
8								33							
9								34							
10								35							
11								36							
12								37							
13								38							
14								39							
15								40							
16								41							
17								42							
18								43							
19								44							
20								45							
21								46							
22								47							
23								48							
24								49							
25								50							
Total								Total							
%								%							

Total Observations

Total Productive

Total Non-productive

% Productive

% Non-productive

Appendix II:

Redesign for Profit

The company that was used in Chapter 12 as an example of a firm that pays proper attention to cost reduction distributes an internal publication to all salaried employees providing instructions on cost reduction techniques and on the company's team system. Appendixes II and III excerpt two sections from the booklet.

In order to either attain or maintain a competitive advantage on major product models, the redesign-for-profit phase is included in the cost reduction program. This phase shall operate as follows:

1. The redesign-for-profit team shall include the manufacturing manager, vice-president of engineering, design engineer, process engineer, tool engineer, foreman, and purchasing manager.

2. The manufacturing manager shall be the team leader. The alternate team leader shall be the vice-president of engineering.

3. Other employees may be added to the team at the request of the team leader.

4. Use of purchased assistance shall require the approval of the division president.

5. The team shall be in session as required until the redesign is completed on schedule to meet the shipping date.

6. The product model to be redesigned shall be selected on the basis of maximum potential yield.

7. At least six product models shall be subjected to redesign for profit each year.

8. The accounting department shall determine price effect of the product changes.

9. As a minimum, the product model review shall include the following:
   (a) Material change to reduce cost
   (b) Reduction in the number of parts in subassemblies
   (c) Parts standardization
   (d) Specify maximum tolerances
   (e) Standardize dimension
   (f) Simplify test and adjustment procedure

10. The design to cost checklist follows and can be used as an idea source list.

Design to Cost Checklist

1. Are all the specification requirements necessary or desirable? (Or do they ask for more than is needed?)

2. Is the hardware's function clearly understood?

3. Does the design provide only what is required in the specifications?

4. Is the design as simple as possible and does it provide only essential functions?

5. Has standard or existing hardware been utilized to the fullest extent?

6. Are test requirements too stringent?

7. Are tolerances and finishes substantially contributing to the cost of the product?

8. Can alternate material be used to reduce costs?

9. Can the design be changed to minimize use of special tooling or equipment?

10. Have newly developed manufacturing techniques been considered for potential cost advantage?

11. Do you have a standard item that can be satisfactorily substituted for this part?

12. Can you suggest any design change that will lower the cost of the item?

13. Do you have any other suggestions that will reduce the cost of this part?

14. Would the cost of the hardware be reduced if the customer provided standard hardware and materials, and performed processing operations?

15. Make an entire subassembly smaller, reducing material accordingly.

16. When buying adjacent parts from vendor, have them preassembled if practical.

17. Make as many parts as practical on a particular job of identical raw material.

18. Design part and tools to hold scrap in machining to a minimum.

19. Provide proper tooling to eliminate need of expensive labor.

20. Avoid complicated equipment that requires continuous scrutiny and maintenance.

21. Check it against other methods of fabrication.

22. Check it against unique, less well-known methods of fabrication.

23. Check unusual but available forms of raw materials for use on the job.

24. Have the suppliers' engineers been given sufficient facts and pressed for suggestions that would produce equivalent performance at lower cost?

25. Should minor changes suggested by the supplier that would afford lower-cost material be considered further?

26. Are parts obtained in best economical lot sizes?

27. Would a relaxation of any tolerances result in lower manufacturing cost?

28. Can you suggest any design changes that will lower the cost of the item?

29. Is there any part of this item that can be more economically produced (considering tooling, etc.) by casting, forging, extruding, or other processes?

30. Can you suggest any material substitute?

31. Are there any finish requirements that could be eliminated or relaxed?

32. Are there any test or qualification requirements that appear unnecessary?

33. Have you any other suggestions that might save weight, simplify the part, or reduce the cost?

34. Do you have a standard item that can be satisfactorily substituted for this part? Is it qualified? What does it cost? What would qualification cost?

35. Can the design be changed to eliminate the purpose of operation?

36. Does everyone concerned know precisely what the inspection requirements are?

37. Are tolerance, allowance, finish, and other requirements necessary?

38. Will lowering the requirements reduce costs materially?

39. Are all tolerances used in actual practice the same as on the drawing?

40. Can material be purchased in sizes that would facilitate handling?

41. Can the design be changed to eliminate or simplify the operation?

42. Is the design of the part suitable to good manufacturing practices?

43. Can equivalent results be obtained at lower cost by design change?

44. Can a standard part be substituted?

45. Can a standard part be converted to do the necessary job?

46. If part is a casting, can it be made lighter by additional coring?

47. Does design of part present difficulties when casting?

48. Can a form cutter perform two or three operations on a certain job at one time more economically than performing these operations separately?

49. Can be so designed as to be suitable for more than one job?

50. Is the activity of the piece sufficient to justify the development of highly specialized tools and fixtures?

51. Can special tools be applied to do more than one operation at a time?

52. Can magazine feed be used?

53. Is the design of the fixture correct?

54. Could higher-cost tooling be justified by increasing order quantity?

55. Does the material specified appear suitable for the purpose for which it is to be used?

56. Could a less expensive material be substituted that would function as well?

57. Could a lighter gauge material be used?

58. Could the supplier perform additional work upon the material that would make it better suited for its use?

59. If a casting or forging, is the excess stock sufficient for machining purposes but not excessive?

60. Can the machinability of the material be improved by heat treatment or in other ways?

61. If a more expensive material that was easier to machine were substituted, would there be a savings?

62. Could the parting of the patterns be changed to eliminate a machining operation on the casting?

63. Could molded or cast parts be substituted to eliminate machining or other operations?

64. Can design be changed to eliminate excessive loss of scrap material?

65. Can newly developed materials be used?

66. If the material is obtainable with reasonable tolerances and surface finish, is it possible to specify a stock size that will eliminate a machining operation?

67. Can extruded material be used?

68. Is the supplier performing assembly operation on a part or material that we later dismantle?

Appendix III:

Elements of Participation in Cost Reduction Teams

This second excerpt from the model company's internal cost reduction booklet describes the individual cost reduction teams.

Organization

1. All salaried employees shall be assigned to a cost improvement team.

2. A staff member or major department manager shall be assigned

3. To the extent practical, cost improvement team members shall be related by department assignment or job content.

4. There shall be nine cost improvement teams, and each team shall average about seven members.

5. Team captains in their cost improvement function shall report to the division president.

6. The division president shall appoint a cost improvement administrator from the division staff.

Goal

Each cost improvement team shall be assigned a monetary goal to be realized in the current calendar year.

Functions of the Cost Improvement Coordinator

1. Insure an adequate supply of cost reduction dockets.

2. Maintain a log of cost reduction dockets (cost improvement control sheet).

3. Route the cost reduction docket to all department managers impacted by the cost reduction suggestion.

4. Insure timely evaluation of the cost reduction suggestion.

5. Prepare and distribute a monthly summary of the cost improvement program (cost improvement docket summary).

6. Prepare and distribute a quarterly list of all salaried employees ranked in order of credited annualized cost improvement dollars.

7. Select and distribute recognition items.

Mechanics

1. Employees shall submit cost improvement suggestions by completing cost improvement docket.

2. The net savings in labor and material dollars shall be calculated on the basis of the controller's assignment of a rate to be used for labor hours and actual material cost savings.

3. All cost improvement suggestions must identify real, tangible, savings.

4. The cost improvement docket shall be routed to the cost improvement coordinator for processing.

Meeting Frequency

Each cost improvement team shall meet weekly. The meeting frequency of teams who are on schedule toward meeting their goal shall be determined by the team captain.

Recognition

1. Each accepted cost improvement suggestion shall be recognized with a certificate presented to the originator.

2. Additional recognition items shall be awarded employees who reach milestones of five, ten, fifteen, and twenty accepted cost improvement suggestions.

3. Each team member shall be awarded a recognition item when all members of that team have an accepted cost improvement to their credit.

4. At a frequency determined by the coordinator, a prize shall be selected and presented at the Management Club meeting on the basis of a selection limited to employees who have been credited with an accepted cost improvement suggestion in the prior month.

5. It is division policy that an accepted cost improvement suggestion is a necessary condition (not a sufficient condition in itself) for a salaried employee merit increase.

Index